BEER AND GOOD FOOD

BY MYRA WALDO

Beer and Good Food

Serve at Once

The Complete Round-the-World Cookbook

Dining Out in Any Language

The Slenderella Cookbook

1001 Ways to Please a Husband

CO-AUTHOR

The Molly Goldberg Cookbook

WITH MOLLY GOLDBERG

BEER

and Good Food

MYRA WALDO

*Brighten your Menus and Recipes
with Beer and Ale*

Doubleday & Company Inc., Garden City, New York, 1958

Contents

Introduction

BEER AND GOOD FOOD *is the result of years of travel and pleasurable research.*

Beer is the most universal beverage in the world. In many countries, beer is used not only as the favorite drink but also as a cooking ingredient.

This book offers you the pleasures of both—beer in food and food with beer.

MYRA WALDO

Beer Isn't New

BEER ISN'T NEW

It would appear likely that soon after man learned to till the soil and harvest its produce he accidentally stumbled upon the fermentation process and learned that crushed grains mixed with water produced a primitive form of beer.

The origin of beer is customarily traced to Mesopotamia and Egypt, the twin cradles of civilization. The earliest written evidence of the brewing process appears on a Mesopotamian clay tablet (believed to be 6200 years old) depicting two men stirring the contents of a brewery vat. Beer isn't specifically mentioned in the Bible, but numerous biblical references to wine are believed to have actually been concerned with beer, for "wine" was then a generic term covering all fermented beverages. To support this, an Assyrian tablet unearthed in the ruins of ancient Nineveh lists beer among the provisions of Noah's ark. A small wooden model of a brewery dating back to about 2000 B.C. was discovered in the tomb of Meket-

Re at Thebes. In 1911, a tightly stoppered jug actually containing
original beer mash made during the Roman occupation was discovered in Alzey, Germany. As the occupation occurred about
sixteen centuries ago, the beer was rather mature.

The ancient Babylonians deemed brewing such an important
part of their economic and social life that they designated two goddesses, Ninkasi and Siris, to watch over it. It may be assumed that
the goddesses co-operated wholeheartedly, for Babylonian beer was
highly regarded (by Babylonians). As far back as 2200 B.C. some
eighteen different varieties of beer were being brewed—dark beer,
red beer, spiced beer, sweet beer, foamy, flat, and with hosts of other
variations. Certain types were reserved exclusively for temple cere-
monies. Anu, god of the sky, was accustomed to receive offerings
of four different kinds of beer in the Temple of Uruk. Was this,
then, an early form of nectar for the gods? Although beer was obviously a drink fit for the gods, lesser types were available to mortal
man.

Babylonian taverns were maintained exclusively by women (ap-
parently the world's first barmaids), with charges and payments
recorded on wet clay tablets. Guests drank on credit, accounts being
settled after each harvest, an early form of Diner's Club charge
accounts. King Hammurabi, author of the world's oldest surviving
code of law, regulated the sale of beer in the interest of consumers
and imposed penalties on delinquent tavern keepers. The punish-
ment for short measure was drowning, a fairly severe penalty but
obviously one that would prevent a repetition of the offense.
Against these risks must be set the rewards; a girl named Ku-Bau,
the forerunner of all barmaids who married well, founded a royal
dynasty at Kish in 3100 B.C. It has been written that Ku-Bau had a
winning smile.

In many old tablets the Babylonians are shown sipping beer
through slim reeds or tubes, the royal family using long straws
made of solid gold which reached from the throne to a container of
beer alongside. While this may have been convenient and restful,
the king missed the pleasure of gazing at the lovely amber-colored
liquid and the delightful sensation of touching his lips to the snowy

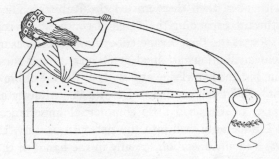

head of foam. One such golden straw, originally the personal sipper of Queen Shu-bad of Mesopotamia, is now at the Museum of the University of Pennsylvania.

In the somewhat similar culture of Egypt, beer, too, had important social and religious connotations. It was the national drink of the country, a basic part of the diet of the rich and the poor, the nobility and the *fellaheen*, the peasant. Beer had already become a convivial beverage and people gathered during the evening for a friendly drink at a local "house of beer." Egyptians were also the first to make beer with bitter herbs, just as we now use hops to add that distinctive irresistible taste.

The nature goddess, Isis, was Egypt's patroness of brewing, and an important official, the "superintendent of breweries," was charged with maintaining the quality of the national beer, as it was an integral part of everyday life and religion. The Egyptians always provided food and beer for those who had departed this life, for how else could they live on in the hereafter? There is an old Egyptian tomb that bears the inscription "Satisfy his spirit . . . with beef and fowl, bread and beer." The men in the taverns raised their goblets with the favorite toast: "Here's beer to your ghost!" But they drank it themselves.

It was the Egyptians who instructed the Greeks in the brewing process, and then the Greeks taught the Romans, who in turn educated the British. The Greeks thought highly of beer, and Sophocles recommended "bread, meat, vegetables, and beer" as an ideal diet; modern dietitians could find no fault with his recommendation today. About 350 years after Sophocles, Julius Caesar toasted his officers with beer when they crossed the Rubicon. The Romans went northward, expanding their area of conquest, capturing Britain, and showed the then savage tribes how to brew beer.

Ancient civilizations attained great heights and subsequently fell to ruin, but the knowledge and skills of the art of brewing continued throughout the centuries. Despite its antiquity and widespread usage, brewing had little commercial importance even in medieval Europe until well into the sixteenth century. Until that time it was a family operation, usually in the hands of the women of the household.

When the monasteries took to brewing beer, it became such an important source of revenue that the people in many communities were forbidden to brew their own until the monastery supply was exhausted. This seldom happened, so the monasteries created a monopoly. Almost every monastery had its own brewhouse, even the stern, unswerving order of the Dominicans. Each brotherhood prepared its beer somewhat differently, the formulas being shrouded in mystery and closely guarded. Some of the monks became as famous for their beer as today's Trappists are for their cheese and the Benedictines for their liqueurs.

In England, according to the Domesday Book, the monastery attached to St. Paul's Cathedral produced more than sixty thousand gallons of ale, of extremely high alcoholic strength, each year.

The ale of Canterbury, in particular, was renowned throughout England for its many virtues: certainly thousands upon thousands of gallons flowed regularly down monkish throats in the Cathedral Priory. There can be no doubt whatsoever that brewing was warm and arduous work, for the allowance of beer was two gallons per monk per day. Thirsty work, that beer brewing!

English ale became the basis for all religious and social festivals, which usually continued unabated until the ale gave out. There were give-ales and bid-ales, almost indistinguishable from our present-day charity bazaars. These were invariably staged to raise money

for some deserving person or, in any event, for some person who had arranged to be the beneficiary of the event. There were lamb-ales, Whitsun-ales, clerk-ales, and as many other ales as there were individuals, groups, guilds, or crafts that had enough beer (or money) to plan the affair. The word "bridal" comes from the bride-ale, the wedding feast. Oxford and Cambridge were famous for their many ales and, yes, held their own college-ales.

While the monks of medieval England were making ale famous, the Germans began using hops to flavor their beer. Hops are vines having a flower with a delightful aroma; it is the dried flower cones of the female plant that are used in brewing. It was at this time that the German word *Bier* came into common usage to distinguish beer (with hops) from ale (without hops). Until that time, a flavoring herb called "gruit" (bog myrtle) had been used; it took almost a hundred years of maneuvering to lift a ban placed on the use of hops by a group of powerful politicians. It appeared that the politicians thought hops completely unsuitable for brewing, and besides, it just so happened they had a monopoly on the production and sale of bog myrtle.

A second German discovery that revolutionized the beer trade was the practice of aging beer instead of selling it immediately after production. It soon became known as lager, from the German *lagern*, meaning "to store." Lager beer may be stored for varying periods up to a year, in order to give it a more subtle, sophisticated flavor. It is the undisputed favorite of beers in the United States today.

During the era of exploration of the American continent, beer was deemed essential in provisioning ships. Water, of course, soon became undrinkable on a long trip, whereas beer remained wholesome for long periods. Beer's nutritive values also helped to ward off many of the diet-deficiency ills to which passengers on long voyages were subject. When Columbus landed on these shores, he found the natives making a first-rate brew, as he wrote "of maize, resembling English beer," and that was the ultimate praise in those days. Almost all Caribbean tribes made beer and drank it regularly, and as with the continental Europeans, brewing was the exclusive responsibility of women, although the men graciously drank it.

The dwindling supply of beer on board the *Mayflower* was a determining factor in the Pilgrims' decision to settle in New England. The original destination was the Virginia Colony, but a journal of the voyage records: "We could not now take time for further search . . . our victuals being much spente, especially our beer."

Colonial Americans were hardy, vigorous people, and beer was on their tables as regularly as bread. A brewhouse was regarded as essential to every household or settlement, depending upon the prosperity of the people. Beer brewed at home was termed "small beer," to distinguish it from the much grander "strong beer," the professional brewer's product; there was also a difference in the strength and body of the respective brews. One of the first breweries in America was established in 1612 in the Dutch colony of New Amsterdam, now sometimes called New York. It was a building where the settlers could make their own beer with their own ingredients, an early do-it-yourself affair. Within a few years so many brewhouses were erected in the community that one street was named *Brouer Street* (Brewer Street).

In 1637 the exclusive right to maintain a brewery was granted to Captain Robert Sedgwick, about whom little is known but who obviously had excellent connections. The same colony in 1634 fixed the price of beer at "one pence a quart at the most." But it wasn't the most; in fact, it was the least, for five years later the price was raised to twopence.

Every encouragement was made by the colonies and subsequently by the states to encourage local breweries. James Madison, in the first Congress, pleaded for a high duty on imported beer to support domestic efforts. The Massachusetts Legislature in 1789 passed an act exempting brewers from taxation for a five-year period, stating that "the wholesome qualities of malt liquors recommend them to general use, as an important means of preserving the health of the citizens of this commonwealth." Following their neighbor's lead, New Hampshire followed with even more liberal legislation.

Perhaps the most famous of all brewers in early American history was Samuel Adams, "Father of the Revolution" and a great defender of liberty. Other distinguished Americans—Thomas Jefferson, James Madison, and Alexander Hamilton—fostered laws to protect the infant industry. Patrick Henry, who worked in his father's tavern, called American taverns "the cradle of liberty," for the revolutionists frequently gathered there to make plans. William Penn, who brought the Quaker faith to this country, had his own private brewery. George Washington's personal recipe for beer, in his own handwriting, is among the prizes in the rare manuscript section of the New York Public Library.

Further great advances in brewing were made by Louis Pasteur, whose discoveries led to the control of the fermentation process during the 1870s. Pasteur must be credited with the discoveries that led to pasteurization, which made beer bottling commercially feasible. Electric refrigeration (which permits longer, more controlled aging) and air conditioning (which sterilizes the air in the fermentation room) also aided the industry greatly. A brewer was responsible for the use of refrigerated railroad cars. Improvements in canning gradually brought about beer in cans, an innovation well received by the American public. Since then beer technology has been constantly moving forward in its efforts to produce the light bright beer it is today.

Beer in Your Life

BEER IN YOUR LIFE

Beer has been an accepted element in hundreds of different civilizations over many thousands of years. Sociologists have noted that the survival of a particular custom or practice indicates that it must, of necessity, fulfill some important function. Inasmuch as beer has persisted successfully, what function does it fulfill?

Five thousand years ago beer was probably the only drink that could be consumed without danger, for water was often contaminated. Subsequently it was used in drought or desert areas because of its keeping qualities; it was also suitable for long sea voyages, during which water became brackish and undrinkable. But most of all, beer was liked and persisted because it was a delicious drink; that is, beer endured because of its excellence as a beverage. In the over all picture, however, mention should be made that life is often tense, emotional, and unrelaxed. Pressures surround us in our workaday life. A mildly alcoholic beverage like beer has a gentle sedative action which tends to relieve the stresses of everyday existence. A glass or two will often produce a feeling of well-being, of relaxation, that softens and eases the tensions of daily stress in this swiftly paced twentieth century.

Beer is a healthy, wholesome drink. An analysis of an 8-ounce glass of beer (an average of leading brands) shows that it contains:

Protein	1.4 gm.
Fat	0.0 gm.
Carbohydrates	10.6 gm.

Vitamins and minerals:

Calcium	10 mg.
Phosphorus	62 mg.
B_1-Thiamine	12.5 mcgm.
B_2-Riboflavin	25–75 mcgm.
B_6-Pyradoxin	125 mcgm.
Niacin	1500–2500 mcgm.
Pantothenate	125–250 mcgm.

The average American beer may be broken down chemically into the following analysis:

Water 92%
Ethyl alcohol 3.6%
Solids or extracts 4.4%

Beer contains no fats whatsoever, an important fact to those who have become aware of the potential hazards of cholesterol. More and more physicians are prescribing beer for low-calorie dieters because of its satisfying psychological effect. Beer is ideal instead of a cocktail before dinner for those who are watching their weight, because it is so filling. And there is nothing to equal beer immediately before bedtime instead of a high-calorie snack, so often the downfall of an otherwise conscientious dieter. Beer at bedtime produces a more restful night of sleep because of its soporific action in relaxing the nervous system.

Beer is pleasantly moderate in calories. An average of leading manufacturers' products shows that 8 ounces have about 100 to 105 calories. It's the ideal drink for the weight-conscious; 8 ounces of beer lasts a long time during a convivial evening, compared to an ounce of bourbon, rye, or scotch, which have 100 calories each.

Cooking with Beer

COOKING WITH BEER

Cooking with beer is traditional, extending back through the centuries, and yet beer cookery is as modern as tomorrow.

The use of beer as a recipe ingredient lends a subtle variation to many dishes, relieving the everyday sameness of routine foods; often it converts homespun repasts into epicurean delights. It intensifies the flavors of familiar recipes, highlighting gravies, sauces, and meats by supplying an artful and intriguing undertone. Beer improves the texture of pancakes, puddings, and cakes by furnishing a desired lightness and buoyancy.

Beer and ale cookery is a present-day inheritance from many foreign lands. It is particularly interesting to note the wide range of classic dishes, well accepted by accomplished chefs the world over, all prepared with beer as an important and requisite ingredient. The Belgians offer *Boeuf à la Flamande*, beefsteak in a beer sauce; fish in black sauce, *Ryba na Cerno*, comes from Czechoslovakia; Den-

mark is fond of *Øllebrod*, a beer soup; and the Germans like to serve *Bratwurst in Bier*, sausages in beer, although these are merely examples. In American colonial days, beer was widely used in cooking, and the settlers were notably fond of a syrup made with beer and brown sugar and customarily served with pancakes.

Beer, used as a marinade, tenderizes and penetrates meat. When basted with beer, roast meats become attractively glazed, delicately browned, and deliciously flavored.

With the growing interest in food today, exciting new recipes are constantly being developed. It is unimportant whether the beer you use is freshly opened or stale—just be sure there is no head on it, so that the quantity used can be measured accurately. If it's too foamy to measure, stir rapidly, and in a few minutes the foam will subside.

Delicious examples of the use of beer in the culinary art are in the following section. You'll find new horizons of cooking with beer and good food.

APPETIZERS

SAVORY PUFF SHELLS

1 cup beer	½ teaspoon salt
¼ pound butter	4 eggs
1 cup sifted flour	

Preheat oven to 450°.

Bring the beer to a boil; add the butter and let melt. Add all the flour and salt at once. Cook, beating steadily until the mixture forms a ball and leaves the side of the pan. Remove from heat. Add 1 egg at a time, beating well after each addition.

Drop by the teaspoon onto a buttered baking sheet. Bake 10 minutes, then reduce heat to 350° and bake 10 minutes longer, or until browned. Cool. Split and fill with pâté, egg mixture, or any cocktail spread.

Makes about 36 1-inch puffs.

APPETIZER TURNOVERS

2 cups sifted flour	½ pound butter
½ teaspoon salt	5 tablespoons sour cream

Sift the flour and salt into a bowl; work in the butter by hand. Add the sour cream, mixing by hand until a dough is formed. Form into a ball and chill for 3 hours. Divide dough in thirds and roll out as thin as possible on a lightly floured surface. Cut into 3-inch rounds or squares. Place a heaping teaspoon of one of the following fillings on each and fold over, sealing the edges well. Arrange on a baking sheet.

Bake in a 400° oven 15 minutes, or until browned.

Makes about 60, depending on how thin you roll the dough.

SEAFOOD FILLING

2 tablespoons butter	¾ cup mashed potatoes
2 tablespoons flour	1 egg yolk
¼ cup heavy cream	1 cup flaked crab meat or
½ cup beer	lobster
¾ teaspoon salt	
¼ teaspoon freshly ground black pepper	

Melt the butter in a saucepan; stir in the flour, mixing until smooth. Gradually add the cream mixed with the beer. Cook over low heat, mixing steadily to the boiling point. Add the salt and pepper. Cook 5 minutes. Beat in the potatoes, then the egg yolk. Cook over low heat, stirring steadily, until mixture bubbles. Add the seafood. Taste for seasoning. Cool, then proceed as directed.

CURRIED MEAT FILLING

1 clove garlic, minced	1 tablespoon curry powder
½ cup chopped onion	2 tablespoons butter
1 tablespoon salad oil	2 tablespoons flour
½ pound ground beef	¼ cup milk
1½ teaspoons salt	½ cup beer

Sauté the garlic and onion in the oil for 10 minutes, stirring frequently. Remove the onions. Brown the meat in the oil remaining in the pan, stirring almost constantly. Season with the salt and curry powder.

Melt the butter in a saucepan; stir in the flour, then the milk mixed with the beer. Cook over low heat, stirring steadily to the boiling point. Cook 5 minutes. Stir in the onions and meat. Taste for seasoning; the mixture should be quite spicy.

SHRIMP SPREAD

1½ pounds raw shrimp	½ cup chopped green or
1½ teaspoons salt	red pepper
2 cups beer	¼ cup grated coconut
1 bay leaf	¼ cup heavy cream
2 tablespoons chopped onion	⅛ teaspoon Tabasco
4 tablespoons watercress	2 tablespoons lemon juice

Wash and drain the shrimp; combine in a saucepan with the salt, beer, and bay leaf. Bring to a boil and cook over low heat 6 minutes. Cool for 10 minutes in the stock. Drain, shell, and devein the shrimp.

If you have a blender, use it to make a purée of the combined shrimp, onion, watercress, pepper, coconut, cream, Tabasco sauce, and lemon juice. If you haven't one, chop the ingredients to a smooth paste. Taste for seasoning. Serve with toast.

Makes about 2 cups.

SAUSAGE BLANKETS

Cook as many small pork sausages as you'll require in beer for 10 minutes. Drain and cool. Prepare pastry or biscuit dough and roll it very thin. Cut in squares. Spread with prepared mustard and chopped onion. Wrap the sausages in it. Brush with egg yolk.

Bake in a 425° oven 15 minutes, or until browned. Serve hot or cold, but they're better hot.

VIENNESE CHEESE SPREAD

1 pound cream cheese	⅛ teaspoon dry mustard
¼ pound butter	1 tablespoon chopped
¼ cup sour cream	chives or scallions
¼ cup beer	1 tablespoon chopped capers
1 teaspoon paprika	1 teaspoon caraway seeds

Beat together the cream cheese, butter, sour cream, and beer. Blend in the paprika, mustard, chives, capers, and caraway seeds. Turn into a bowl or shape into a mound. Chill. Serve with pumpernickel or crackers.

STUFFED EDAM CHEESE

1 small Edam cheese	½ teaspoon dry mustard
¼ pound butter	2 tablespoons grated onion
1 cup beer	½ cup chopped stuffed olives

Cut a 2-inch piece from the top of an Edam cheese; carefully scoop out the inside. You may grind the cheese in a food chopper or cream it in an electric mixer with the butter. Beat in the beer, adding just enough to make a smooth, spreadable mixture. Beat in the mustard, onion, and olives. Stuff the Edam shell and chill until ready to serve with toast or crackers.

PIQUANT CHEESE SPREAD (*Bier Kase*)

¾ pound Cheddar cheese	½ teaspoon dry mustard
⅛ pound Roquefort cheese	¼ teaspoon salt
2 tablespoons butter	¾ cup ale or beer
2 teaspoons grated onion	
½ teaspoon Worcestershire sauce	

Grate the Cheddar cheese and crumble the Roquefort cheese into a bowl; add the butter, onion, Worcestershire sauce, mustard, and salt. Cream together with an electric mixer or wooden spoon, then gradually add the ale or beer, mixing until smooth. Pack into crocks or jars and cover tightly. Refrigerate until needed. Serve with thinly sliced bread. A small pumpernickel hollowed out and filled with the cheese spread is an attractive way to serve it. Makes about 3 cups.

CHEESE LOG

½ pound Roquefort cheese	2 tablespoons grated onion
½ pound cream cheese	½ cup minced black olives
4 tablespoons butter	¾ cup chopped toasted nuts
2 tablespoons beer	

Cream together the Roquefort, cream cheese, and butter. Blend in the beer, onion, and olives, mixing until smooth.

Shape into a 1-inch-thick log and roll in the nuts; chill. Slice with a very sharp wet knife and place on crackers or rounds of toast.

CHEESE CANAPÉS

3 tablespoons butter	½ pound (2 cups) grated
2 tablespoons grated onion	Gruyère or Swiss cheese
3 tablespoons flour	¼ cup beer
1½ teaspoons salt	1 egg yolk, beaten
¼ teaspoon pepper	8 slices toasted white bread,
Dash cayenne pepper	trimmed and cut in tri-
1 cup milk	angles

Melt the butter in a saucepan; blend in the onion, flour, salt, pepper, and cayenne, stirring until golden. Gradually add the milk, stirring constantly to the boiling point. Cook over low heat 5 minutes. Add the cheese and beer, stirring until cheese melts. Beat in the egg yolk.

Spread the mixture on the toast triangles, leaving a small border all around to prevent running over. Arrange on a baking sheet.

Bake in a 450° oven 5 minutes, or until browned.

CHEESE TWIRLS

2 cups sifted flour	⅔ cup shortening
1 teaspoon salt	1 cup grated American cheese
2 teaspoons curry powder	⅓ cup beer

Sift the flour, salt, and curry powder into a bowl. Cut in the shortening and cheese until well blended. Add the beer gradually, tossing until a ball of dough is formed. (It may not be necessary to add all the beer.) Chill for ½ hour. Preheat oven to 425°.

Roll out the dough ⅛ inch thick. Cut into strips 4 inches long and ½ inch wide. Twirl the pastry 3 times. Arrange on a baking sheet.

Bake 10 minutes or until delicately browned. Cool and keep in an airtight container until needed. Delicious as an hors d'oeuvre or with soup.

*   *   *

Bryng us in no befe, for ther is many bonys
But bryng us in good ale, for that goes down at onys
Bryng us in no eggys, for ther is many schelles
But bryng us in good ale, and gyfe us nothyng ellys.
  Anonymous, Bryng Us in Good Ale (*Old drinking song of the fifteenth century*)

CHEESE TART (Salé)

3 tablespoons butter	½ cup heavy cream
2 tablespoons grated onion	3 eggs, beaten
3 tablespoons flour	1¼ cups grated Gruyère or
1 teaspoon salt	Swiss cheese
¼ teaspoon nutmeg	9-inch unbaked pie shell
1 cup beer	

Melt the butter in a saucepan; stir in the onion. Cook over low heat 2 minutes. Blend in the flour, salt, and nutmeg; gradually add the beer and cream. Cook over low heat, stirring constantly to the boiling point. Cool 10 minutes. Preheat oven to 400°.

Add the eggs and cheese to the beer sauce. Taste for seasoning. Turn into the pie shell.

Bake 30 minutes or until browned and set.

SOUPS

BLACK FOREST BEER SOUP

1 egg yolk	1 cup sour cream
1 teaspoon flour	6 cups beer
½ teaspoon salt	6 slices garlic toast
Dash cayenne pepper	¾ cup grated Gruyère cheese

Beat the egg yolk, flour, salt, cayenne pepper, and sour cream together in a bowl. Bring the beer to a boil and add to the sour cream mixture, stirring constantly to prevent curdling. Reheat, but do not allow to boil.

Place a slice of toast in each soup bowl and sprinkle with cheese.

Serves 6.

COLD CUCUMBER SOUP, FINNISH STYLE

1½ cups beer	1 teaspoon salt
1½ cups sour cream	¼ teaspoon freshly ground
2 cucumbers, peeled and diced	black pepper

Gradually add the beer to the sour cream, stirring well. Add the cucumbers, salt and pepper. Stir and taste for seasoning. Serve very cold.

Serves 4.

CANADIAN CHEESE SOUP

3 tablespoons minced onion	2 tablespoons cornstarch
3 tablespoons grated carrot	¼ cup milk
3 tablespoons butter	¼ pound (1 cup) grated
4 cups chicken broth	Cheddar cheese
½ teaspoon dry mustard	1 cup beer
½ teaspoon paprika	2 tablespoons minced parsley

Cook the onion and carrot in the butter for 10 minutes, stirring occasionally. Add the broth, mustard, and paprika. Cook over low heat 15 minutes. Mix together the cornstarch and milk; stir into the soup. Cook 5 minutes. Add the cheese and beer, stirring over low heat until cheese melts. Taste for seasoning. Sprinkle with the parsley. Serves 6.

*   *   *

When Queen Elizabeth traveled across her realm a beer taster was sent ahead to check the local supply. If it proved inferior, the Queen's Own was rushed to her from London.

*   *   *

DANISH BEER SOUP (Øllebrod)

1 quart beer	1 tablespoon butter
1 quart water	3 egg yolks
3 tablespoons sugar	1 cup heavy cream

Combine the beer, water, sugar, and butter in a saucepan. Bring to a boil and cook over low heat 15 minutes.

Beat together the egg yolks and cream. Gradually add the beer mixture, stirring steadily to prevent curdling. Reheat, but do not let boil. Serve with croutons.

Serves 6.

LENTIL SOUP

1½ cups lentils	1 cup canned tomatoes
½ cup diced onions	2 teaspoons salt
¼ cup sliced celery	¼ teaspoon pepper
2 tablespoons butter	1 cup beer
6 cups water	1 cup diced potatoes

Wash the lentils thoroughly. Sauté the onions and celery in the butter for 10 minutes. Add the water, tomatoes, salt, pepper, and lentils. Cover loosely and cook over low heat 2 hours. Force through a sieve or purée in an electric blender. Return to the saucepan and add the beer and potatoes. Cook 20 minutes. Taste for seasoning.   Serves 6–8.

BELGIAN ONION SOUP

4 cups thinly sliced onions	3 cups beer
4 tablespoons butter	3 cups beef broth
1 teaspoon salt	2 tablespoons cornstarch
1 teaspoon sugar	½ cup light cream

Sauté the onions in the butter for 20 minutes, stirring frequently. Add the salt, sugar, beer, and broth. Cook over low heat 40 minutes. Mix the cornstarch and cream until smooth; add to the soup, stirring constantly to the boiling point. Cook over low heat 5 minutes.   Serves 6.

FARM-STYLE LEEK SOUP

6 leeks, thinly sliced	⅛ teaspoon minced garlic
2 onions, minced	1 cup medium noodles
4 tablespoons butter	1 cup grated Swiss cheese
5 cups chicken consommé	1 cup beer

Sauté the leeks and onions in the butter over low heat for 15 minutes. (Stir frequently to prevent browning.) Stir in the consommé and garlic; cover and cook over low heat 30 minutes.

Cook the noodles half as long as package directs; drain and add to the soup. Cook 5 minutes. Taste for seasoning.

Melt the cheese over hot water and gradually add the beer. Divide the cheese mixture among 6 soup cups and pour the soup over it.

Serves 6.

CABBAGE SOUP

3 tablespoons butter
3 pounds cabbage, finely shredded
4 cups chicken consommé
½ teaspoon freshly ground black pepper

2 cups beer
2 tablespoons flour
1 cup heavy cream

Melt the butter in a saucepan; cook the cabbage in it over low heat for 20 minutes, stirring frequently. Add the consommé, pepper, and beer. Cover loosely and cook over low heat 1 hour.

Mix together the flour and cream; add to the soup, stirring constantly to the boiling point. Cook over low heat 10 minutes; taste for seasoning. Serve with cheese sticks.

Serves 6–8.

*   *   *

Old records going back to the fifteenth century show that almost half of the ships' cargoes across the North and Baltic seas consisted of barrels of beer.

FISH AND SHELLFISH

BIER FISCH

6 slices carp (about 3 pounds)
1 tablespoon salt
1 cup diced onions
2½ cups beer
1 bay leaf

½ teaspoon freshly ground black pepper
3 slices lemon
2 tablespoons sugar
6 gingersnaps, crushed
1 tablespoon butter

Wash and drain the fish; sprinkle with the salt. Set aside for 15 minutes. In a deep skillet, spread the onions and arrange the carp over them. Add the beer, bay leaf, pepper, lemon, and sugar. Bring to a boil; cover loosely and cook over low heat 30 minutes. Transfer the fish to a serving dish. Stir the gingersnaps and butter into the stock and cook over high heat 2 minutes. Taste for seasoning and pour over the fish.
Serves 6–8.

FRIED SOFT-SHELL CRABS

12 soft-shell crabs
2 eggs
1 teaspoon salt
¼ cup beer

½ cup dry bread crumbs
¼ cup flour
½ teaspoon pepper
Fat for deep frying

Have the crabs cleaned by the fishman; wash and dry.
Beat together the eggs, salt, and beer. Mix the bread crumbs,

flour, and pepper. Dip the crabs in the egg mixture and then in the bread-crumb mixture, coating them well.

Heat the fat to 360° and fry 2 or 3 crabs at a time until browned. Drain. Serves 4–6.

FILLET OF SOLE DIABLE

4 fillets of sole
4 tablespoons flour
1 teaspoon salt
¼ teaspoon pepper
2 tablespoons butter

¾ cup beer
1½ teaspoons Worcestershire sauce
½ teaspoon powdered mustard

Dip the fillets in the flour seasoned with the salt and pepper. Melt the butter in a baking dish; arrange the fillets in it. Mix together the beer, Worcestershire sauce, and mustard; pour over the fish.

Bake in a 375° oven 35 minutes, basting frequently. Serves 4.

BAKED CLAMS

4 tablespoons butter
1 tablespoon minced parsley
2 tablespoons grated onion
½ teaspoon minced garlic
¼ cup beer

24 clams on the half shell
8 slices bacon, half cooked and drained
4 tablespoons bread crumbs

Cream the butter, parsley, onion, and garlic together. Gradually beat in the beer. Place a small amount of the mixture on each clam. Cut the bacon in thirds and cover the clams with it. Sprinkle with the bread crumbs. Arrange on a baking pan and bake in a 375° oven for 10 minutes.

Serves 4–6.

FISH IN BLACK SAUCE

2 teaspoons pickling spice
¼ teaspoon thyme
2 bay leaves
2 cloves garlic
2 cups water
1 cup vinegar
½ cup sliced onions
1 stalk celery
6 slices carp, bass, whitefish,
   or pike
2 teaspoons salt

½ teaspoon ground ginger
18 prunes, pitted and
   chopped
¾ cup boiling water
12 gingersnaps, crushed
2 cups beer
2 tablespoons lemon juice
¼ cup sugar
½ cup seedless raisins
½ cup sliced almonds

Place the pickling spice, thyme, bay leaves, and garlic in a piece of cheesecloth and tie it securely. Combine in a deep skillet with the water, vinegar, onions, and celery. Bring to a boil and cook 30 minutes. Add the fish, salt, and ginger. Cook over low heat 30 minutes. Discard the bag of spices.

Meanwhile cook the prunes in the boiling water for 20 minutes. Soak the gingersnaps in the beer and add to the fish along with the lemon juice, sugar, raisins, almonds, and undrained prunes. Cook 10 minutes. Serve hot. Serves 6.

FISH IN BEER SAUCE

6 slices fish (bass, whitefish,
   salmon, trout)
2 teaspoons salt
¼ teaspoon pepper
4 tablespoons butter
4 tablespoons minced onion

2 tablespoons flour
2 cups beer
1 tablespoon sugar
2 cloves
1 tablespoon lemon juice

Wash and dry the fish; sprinkle with the salt and pepper. Melt the butter in a deep skillet; sauté the onion for 5 minutes.

Add the flour, stirring until golden. Gradually add the beer, stirring constantly to the boiling point. Arrange the fish in the sauce and add the sugar and cloves. Cover loosely and cook over low heat 30 minutes. Transfer the fish to a platter; stir the lemon juice into the sauce. Taste for seasoning and pour over the fish.
Serves 6.

SHRIMP RAMEKINS

2 pounds raw shrimp, shelled and deveined	¾ cup beer
	½ cup chopped stuffed olives
½ pound cream cheese	2 tablespoons minced parsley
½ pound blue cheese	

Preheat oven to 400°.
Divide the shrimp among 6 or 8 ramekins or baking dishes. Beat together the cream cheese and blue cheese; gradually stir in the beer and then the olives. Spread over the shrimp. Cover each ramekin with a piece of aluminum foil.
Bake 25 minutes. Remove foil and sprinkle with the parsley.
Serves 6–8.

SOLE WISCONSIN

1½ cups beer	½ teaspoon pepper
¼ cup minced onions	6 egg yolks
2 tablespoons minced parsley	¼ pound butter
6 fillets of sole	2 tablespoons heavy cream
1 teaspoon salt	

Combine the beer, onions, and parsley in a deep skillet; bring to a boil and cook over low heat 5 minutes. Arrange the fillets carefully in the beer mixture; sprinkle with salt and pepper. Cover loosely and cook over low heat 10 minutes, or until fish flakes when tested with a fork.

Carefully transfer the fish to a shallow baking dish and keep warm. Reduce beer mixture to ½ cup.

Beat the egg yolks in the top of a double boiler. Gradually add the beer, mixing steadily. Break the butter into small pieces and add. Place over hot water and cook, beating steadily (with wire whisk or fork) until thickened. Stir in the cream and taste for seasoning; pour over the fish.

Place under a hot broiler until delicately browned. Serve at once.

Serves 6.

FILLET OF SOLE, CHINESE STYLE

4 fillets of sole	⅓ cup cider vinegar
3 egg yolks	½ cup chicken broth
2 tablespoons beer	¼ cup sugar
6 tablespoons cornstarch	2 tablespoons ketchup
½ teaspoon salt	2 tablespoons chopped fresh
½ cup dry bread crumbs	ginger or 1 teaspoon
Fat for deep frying	powdered
¼ cup water	
4 tablespoons peanut or salad oil	

Buy thick fillets and cut each one in half crosswise. Wash and dry. Beat together the egg yolks, beer, 5 tablespoons cornstarch, and the salt. Dip the fish in this mixture and then in the bread crumbs, coating them thoroughly.

Heat the fat to 365° and fry the fillets in it, without crowding, until browned on both sides. Keep the fish hot while preparing the sauce.

Mix the remaining cornstarch with the water and combine in

a saucepan with oil, vinegar, broth, sugar, ketchup, and ginger. Cook over low heat, stirring constantly, until thickened. Taste for seasoning.   Serves 4–6.

AAL IN BIER (*Eel in Beer*)

1½ pounds eel	¼ teaspoon pepper
2 cups beer	2 tablespoons butter
½ cup minced onions	2 tablespoons flour
1 teaspoon salt	2 tablespoons parsley

Wash the eel and skin it carefully; cut into 1-inch pieces. Combine the beer, onions, salt, and pepper in a saucepan; bring to a boil and add the eel. Cook over low heat 20 minutes. Transfer the eel to a serving dish. Knead the butter and flour together and add to the beer stock; cook over low heat, stirring constantly until sauce thickens. Pour over the eel. Sprinkle with the parsley.

Serves 6–8.

SHRIMP CREOLE

1½ pounds raw shrimp, shelled and deveined	½ cup diced onions
½ cup flour	1½ cups beer
1 teaspoon salt	1 cup canned tomato sauce
¼ teaspoon pepper	1 teaspoon sugar
3 tablespoons butter	1 bay leaf

Wash and drain the shrimp. Dip in a mixture of the flour, salt, and pepper. Melt the butter in a skillet and lightly brown the shrimp and onions. Add the beer, tomato sauce, sugar, and bay leaf; bring to a boil and cook 10 minutes. Taste for seasoning. Serve with fluffy boiled rice.

Serves 4–6.

SPANISH LOBSTER SALAD

4 cups beer	2 cups cooked, diced potatoes
2 cups water	2 cups cooked or canned peas
2 teaspoons salt	2 cups shredded lettuce
1 bay leaf	½ teaspoon saffron
1 onion	1 tablespoon lemon juice
2 live lobsters or 4 lobster tails	1½ cups mayonnaise

Combine the beer, water, salt, bay leaf, and onion. Bring to a boil and plunge the lobsters into it. Cover and cook over medium heat 20 minutes. Cool in the liquid for 30 minutes. Split the lobsters and dice the meat.

In a large bowl combine the lobster, potatoes, peas, and lettuce. Taste for seasoning. Chill.

Dissolve the saffron in the lemon juice and add to the mayonnaise. Pour over the salad and toss lightly. Serves 6–8.

SPICED SHRIMP BOWL

2 pounds raw shrimp, shelled and deveined	1½ cups beer
2 tablespoons olive or salad oil	1 teaspoon dry mustard
	1 teaspoon celery seed
1½ teaspoons salt	¼ teaspoon dried, ground red peppers
½ teaspoon freshly ground black pepper	

Wash and drain the shrimp. Heat the oil in a skillet; sauté the shrimp for 1 minute on each side. Sprinkle with the salt and pepper. Bring the beer, mustard, celery seed, and red pepper to a boil; pour over the shrimp. Cook over medium heat 5 minutes. Cool, then let shrimp marinate in sauce for 24 hours. Drain and pierce shrimp with cocktail picks.

SHRIMP, NORTH SEA FASHION

2 pounds raw shrimp	⅛ teaspoon thyme
3 cups beer	1½ tablespoons cornstarch
¾ teaspoon salt	3 tablespoons water
⅛ teaspoon freshly ground	1 cup cream
black pepper	2 tablespoons butter
1 bay leaf	2 teaspoons minced parsley

Wash, shell, and devein the shrimp, reserving a few shells. Bring the beer, salt, pepper, bay leaf, and thyme to a boil; add the shrimp and shells. Cook over low heat 5 minutes. Remove the shrimp and discard the shells. Reduce the stock to half, about 1½ cups.

Mix the cornstarch and water together and add to the beer stock, stirring constantly until boiling point is reached. Blend in the cream, butter, and parsley. Add the shrimp and reheat. Serve on rice or noodles. Serves 4–6.

LOBSTER, HOLLAND FASHION

4 cups beer	2 tablespoons flour
2 live lobsters or 4 frozen	½ teaspoon salt
lobster tails	¼ teaspoon pepper
2 onions, diced	1 teaspoon caraway seeds
2 tablespoons butter	

Bring the beer to a boil. Add the lobsters and cook 20 minutes. Remove and cool the lobsters; reserve the stock. Remove the meat of the lobsters and dice it.

Melt the butter in a saucepan; stir in the flour, salt, pepper, and caraway seeds. Gradually add the beer stock, stirring constantly to the boiling point. Cook over low heat 5 minutes longer. Strain the sauce and heat the lobster in it. Taste for seasoning.

Serves 4–6 as a first course on toast or 2–3 as a main course.

SHRIMP AND RICE (*Arroz con Camarones*)

2 pounds raw shrimp, shelled and deveined
4 cups beer
2 tablespoons lemon juice
1 teaspoon salt
¼ teaspoon freshly ground black pepper
1 bay leaf
3 tablespoons butter
½ cup diced onion
1 cup uncooked rice
¾ cup diced green pepper
½ pound mushrooms, sliced
2 pimientos, sliced

Wash and drain the shrimp. Combine the shrimp, beer, lemon juice, salt, pepper, and bay leaf. Bring to a boil and cook 5 minutes. Drain, reserving the stock.

Melt the butter in a saucepan. Add the onion and rice; cook over medium heat, stirring almost constantly until lightly browned. Add the reserved stock, green pepper, and mushrooms. Cover and cook over low heat 15 minutes, or until rice is tender. Add the shrimp and pimientos. Taste for seasoning.   Serves 4–6.

LOBSTER AMANDINE

4 tablespoons butter
3 tablespoons flour
1 cup light cream
½ cup milk
½ cup beer
1½ teaspoons salt
¼ teaspoon pepper
2 egg yolks
2 cups cooked, diced lobster
½ cup blanched, sliced almonds

Melt the butter in a saucepan; stir in the flour. Gradually add the cream, milk, and beer, stirring steadily to the boiling point. Cook over low heat 5 minutes.

Lightly beat together the salt, pepper, and egg yolks. Gradually add the sauce, stirring steadily to prevent curdling. Pour back into the saucepan and add the lobster and almonds. Heat but do not let boil. Taste for seasoning. Serve on buttered toast or in patty shells. Serves 6.

POULTRY

CHICKEN WITH RICE (*Arroz con Pollo*)

1 3-pound fryer, disjointed
⅓ cup olive oil
2 onions, chopped
2 cloves garlic, minced
1 green pepper, chopped
½ cup canned tomatoes,
   drained
3 cups chicken consommé

1 cup beer
1 bay leaf
2 teaspoons salt
½ teaspoon saffron
1 cup raw rice
1 cup cooked or canned green
   peas

Use a casserole or Dutch oven and serve directly from it.

Brown the chicken in the oil; remove. In the remaining oil, sauté the onions, garlic, and green pepper for 10 minutes. Return the chicken and add the tomatoes, consommé, beer, bay leaf, salt, and saffron. Cover and cook over low heat 20 minutes. Add the rice; recover and cook 20 minutes. Add the peas and cook 5 minutes longer, or until rice is tender. Garnish with pimientos and olives if desired.

Serves 4–5.

*   *   *

He that eateth well, drinketh well; he that drinketh well, sleepeth well; he that sleepeth well, sinneth not; he that sinneth not goeth straight through purgatory to Paradise.

             William Lithgow (1583–1650)

CHICKEN-BREAD PUDDING (*Budin de Pain*)

6 slices toast, trimmed and
buttered
½ cup chicken consommé
½ cup beer
3 cups minced chicken or
turkey
½ cup grated Parmesan
cheese

2 tablespoons melted butter
½ teaspoon freshly ground
black pepper
2 tablespoons minced parsley
½ cup bread crumbs

Line a buttered baking dish with the toast. Mix the consommé and beer together and pour over the toast.

Mix together the chicken, cheese, butter, pepper, and parsley. Spread the mixture over the toast and sprinkle with the bread crumbs.

Bake in a 375° oven 45 minutes.

Serves 6.

BATTER-FRIED CHICKEN

1 cup sifted flour
1 teaspoon salt
¼ teaspoon pepper
2 eggs
½ cup beer

2 tablespoons melted butter
2½-pound frying chicken,
disjointed
Fat for deep frying

Sift the flour, salt, and pepper into a bowl. Beat the eggs and beer together and add to the flour, mixing until smooth. Stir in the butter. Dip the chicken into the batter, coating the pieces thoroughly. Arrange on a pan and chill 1 hour.

Heat the fat to 360°. Fry the chicken until browned. Arrange on a baking sheet and bake in a 350° oven 35 minutes, or until tender.

Serves 4.

What better on a hot summer day than *Batter-Fried Chicken*
(recipe opposite) and mugs of cool, clear beer or ale.

SPICY COCONUT CHICKEN

2 2½-pound fryers, disjointed
4 tablespoons peanut or salad oil
2 cups finely chopped onions
1 clove garlic, minced
¼ cup ground almonds
1 tablespoon molasses
2 teaspoons salt
½ teaspoon dried, ground chili peppers
1 bay leaf
¾ cup beer
¼ cup heavy cream
½ cup grated coconut

Brown the chicken in the oil; remove. In the oil remaining in the pan sauté the onions and garlic for 10 minutes. Stir in the almonds, molasses, salt, and chili peppers. Return the chicken to the pan and add the bay leaf, beer, cream, and coconut. Cover and cook over low heat 1 hour, or until chicken is tender.
Serves 6–8.

*   *   *

Queen Elizabeth seemed to care for nothing but bread and ale for her breakfast. Records of the household accounts dating back to 1576 show that the Queen drank considerable quantities, but this was in accordance with local custom of the time, which considered beer the ideal breakfast food.

MARINATED FRIED CHICKEN

2 2½-pound frying chickens, disjointed
½ cup olive oil
¼ cup lemon juice
1 cup beer
2 teaspoons salt
¼ teaspoon freshly ground black pepper
3 eggs
2 cups bread crumbs
¾ cup shortening or oil

Wash and dry the chickens. Make a marinade of the oil, lemon juice, beer, 1 teaspoon salt, and the pepper and marinate the chicken for 3–4 hours. Drain.

Beat the eggs and remaining salt together. Dip the chicken first in the eggs and then the bread crumbs, coating the pieces well.

Heat half the shortening in a skillet; fry the chicken over low heat until tender and browned. Add more shortening as needed. Serves 8.

ROAST STUFFED CHICKEN

2 teaspoons salt
½ teaspoon pepper
1 roasting chicken
¼ cup minced onion
2 tablespoons butter
2 cups bread cubes
1 egg, beaten
½ pound ham, ground
2 tablespoons tomato paste
2 tablespoons lemon juice
½ cup orange juice
3 tablespoons olive oil
1 cup beer
1 teaspoon sugar

Rub salt and pepper into the chicken. Sauté the onion in the butter for 5 minutes, stirring frequently. Add the bread cubes, egg, and ham. Mix lightly and taste for seasoning. Stuff the chicken and close the opening with skewers, thread, or aluminum foil. Place in a roasting pan and roast in a 425° oven 20 minutes.

Mix the tomato paste, lemon juice, orange juice, oil, beer, and

sugar together. Pour over the chicken. Reduce the heat to 350°.
Roast 2 hours longer, or until chicken is tender, basting frequently.
Serves 4–6.

BREWER'S CHICKEN SAUTÉ

3 tablespoons butter	¾ cup beer
1 3-pound fryer, disjointed	3 tablespoons canned tomato
12 small white onions	sauce
2 teaspoons salt	1 bay leaf
2 teaspoons paprika	½ cup light cream

Melt the butter in a casserole or deep skillet; brown the chicken
in it. Add the onions and cook until they turn yellow. Sprinkle
with salt and paprika and stir in the beer, tomato sauce, and bay
leaf. Cover and cook over low heat 45 minutes, or until chicken is
tender. Skim the fat; stir in the cream. Discard bay leaf. Heat and
serve.

Serves 4.

DUCK WITH RICE (*Arroz con Pato*)

1 duck (5–6 pounds)	1 teaspoon Spanish paprika
2 tablespoons salad oil	3 cups boiling water
2 cloves garlic, minced	1½ cups raw rice
2 teaspoons salt	1 cup green peas, fresh or
½ teaspoon dried, ground chili	frozen
peppers	½ cup beer

Wash, singe, and dry the duck. Cut into small pieces and remove as much fat as possible.

Heat the oil in a casserole or Dutch oven; brown the duck with
the garlic. Pour off the fat; season the duck with the salt, chili

peppers, and paprika. Add 1 cup of boiling water. Cover and cook over low heat 45 minutes. Add the remaining 2 cups of boiling water and the rice; mix lightly. Cover and cook over low heat 20 minutes; add peas. Cook 10 minutes longer, or until rice is tender and dry. Stir in the beer and taste for seasoning. Cook 5 minutes. Serves 4–5.

BRAISED DUCK

1 duck, disjointed	¾ cup beer
1 tablespoon butter	½ cup chicken stock
2 onions, diced	⅛ teaspoon thyme
3 tablespoons flour	⅛ teaspoon basil

Remove as much fat as possible from the duck. Melt the butter in a casserole and brown the duck. Pour off the fat. Add the onions; cook until brown. Sprinkle with the flour; stir in the beer, stock, thyme, and basil. Cover and cook over low heat 1 hour, or until duck is tender. Skim the fat.

Serves 4.

MEAT

Boeuf à la Flamande, also called *Carbonnades à la Flamande,* is a Belgian dish famous throughout the world. The flavor of the dish, with beer as its base, is so unusual that even the French have adopted it as part of their classic cuisine.

BOEUF À LA FLAMANDE

4 pounds beef (brisket, eye round, chuck)	2 teaspoons salt
	½ teaspoon pepper
4 cups sliced onions	1 teaspoon sugar
4 tablespoons butter	2 bay leaves
2 tablespoons flour	½ teaspoon thyme
2 cups beer	3 tablespoons minced parsley
1 tablespoon vinegar	

Buy first-cut brisket or have the other types cut 1 inch thick. Cut into 12 pieces.

Use a Dutch oven or heavy saucepan and brown the onions in the butter. Remove the onions and brown the meat in the remaining butter. Sprinkle with the flour. Add the onions, beer, vinegar, salt, pepper, sugar, bay leaves, thyme, and parsley. Cover and cook over low heat 3 hours, or until meat is very tender.

Serves 6–8.

*   *   *

Shakespeare's plays are filled with references to beer and ale; his father was an ale taster in Stratford-on-Avon.

SWISS STEAK

3 pounds round steak, 1-inch thick
¾ cup flour
2 teaspoons salt
½ teaspoon pepper
¼ teaspoon garlic powder
3 tablespoons butter

1½ cups beer
2 tablespoons tomato paste
1 bay leaf
1 clove
6 potatoes, pared and halved
12 small white onions

Cut the steak into 6 or 8 serving-size pieces. Season the flour with salt, pepper, and garlic powder; pound it into the steak on both sides with a mallet, cleaver, or knife.

Melt the butter in a Dutch oven or heavy saucepan and brown the steak on both sides. Add the beer, tomato paste, bay leaf, and clove. Cover and cook over low heat 1 hour. Add the potatoes and onions; cook covered 25 minutes, or until vegetables are tender. Taste for seasoning. Discard bay leaf.

Serves 6–8.

MARINATED POT ROAST

1½ cups beer
⅓ cup olive or salad oil
2 tablespoons honey
1 tablespoon salt
¾ teaspoon freshly ground black pepper

4 cloves
4 pounds beef (eye round, cross rib, etc.)
2 tablespoons butter
2 onions, sliced
2 carrots, grated

Combine the beer, oil, honey, salt, pepper and cloves in a bowl. Add the beef and let marinate 12–24 hours or overnight; turn and baste the meat frequently.

Drain the meat, reserving the marinade. Melt the butter in a Dutch oven or heavy saucepan and brown the meat, onions, and carrots. Stir in 1½ cups of the marinade. Cover and cook over low heat 2½ hours, or until tender. Turn the meat once or twice during the cooking time and add the remaining marinade if needed. Serves 8–10.

ROAST PRIME RIBS OF BEEF

6- to 8-pound rib roast	1½ cups beer
1 tablespoon salt	1 tablespoon butter

Buy the first ribs if possible and have them cut short. Rub the meat with the salt and place it in a shallow roasting pan. Insert a meat thermometer if you have one. Roast in a 450° oven 20 minutes; pour off the fat and add the beer. Reduce the heat to 350° and roast 12 minutes more per pound for rare, 15 for medium, and 18 for well done, or until thermometer registers the degree of doneness you want. Baste frequently. Transfer the meat to a platter.

To prepare the gravy, skim the fat from the pan and measure the gravy left. Add enough water to make 1 cup and return to the pan. Cook over low heat, stirring in all the crustiness. Taste for seasoning and stir in the butter. Serves 6–10.

CREOLE BEEF

2 pounds sirloin or round steak, cubed small	½ cup chili sauce
2 onions, sliced	½ cup diced green pepper
2 tablespoons olive oil	½ teaspoon freshly ground black pepper
1½ cups beer	3 cups cooked rice

Brown the steak and onions in the oil. Add the beer, chili sauce, green pepper, and black pepper. Cover and cook over low heat 45 minutes, or until steak is tender. Taste for seasoning. Heap the rice on a heated serving platter and pour the meat over it. Serves 6–8.

* * *

Fifteen hundred years ago only members of the clergy knew how to read—thus even in the twentieth century those who deal with papers are called clerical workers. But everyone could recognize the checkered flag which indicated a place where ale and beer could be purchased.

MUNICH BEEF

3 cups beer	3 tablespoons fat
1 cup minced onions	2 carrots, sliced
1½ teaspoons salt	1 tablespoon flour
¼ teaspoon freshly ground black pepper	2 tablespoons grated orange rind
	2 tablespoons currant jelly
3 pounds round or rump steak cut in 2-inch cubes	1 tablespoon lemon juice

In a bowl, combine the beer, onions, salt, pepper, and steak. Let marinate 12–24 hours or overnight in the refrigerator. Remove the meat from the marinade and drain it well, but reserve the marinade.

Melt the fat in a Dutch oven or heavy saucepan and brown the meat. Add the marinade and carrots; cover and cook over low heat 2½ hours. Mix the flour with a little water and add to the gravy with the orange rind, jelly, and lemon juice. Cook 5 minutes. Serves 6.

BRAISED SHORT RIBS

1 tablespoon butter	2 bay leaves
3 pounds short ribs (cut into 4 pieces)	1 teaspoon sugar
	1 cup beer
¾ cup thinly sliced onions	1 tablespoon cornstarch
1 teaspoon salt	¼ cup water
¼ teaspoon pepper	3 tablespoons heavy cream
½ teaspoon whole allspice	

Melt the butter in a Dutch oven or heavy saucepan and brown the ribs on all sides. Add the onions and cook until browned. Stir in the salt, pepper, allspice, bay leaves, sugar, and beer. Cover and cook over low heat 1½ hours, or until tender. Skim the fat from the gravy.

Mix the cornstarch and water to a smooth paste. Add to the gravy, stirring constantly to the boiling point. Cook over low heat 5 minutes. Stir in the cream and taste for seasoning.

Serves 4.

ANGLO-INDIAN BEEF

2 pounds round or sirloin steak	1 tablespoon curry powder
4 tablespoons butter	½ cup chopped apple
1 cup diced onions	¼ cup grated coconut
1 cup beer	¼ cup ground almonds
1 teaspoon salt	

Have the beef cut thin or pound it. Cut crosswise into very narrow strips.

Melt the butter in a deep skillet and brown the onions. Remove the onions and brown the meat in the skillet. Return the onions and add the beer, salt, and curry powder. Cover and cook over low heat 45 minutes. Add the apple, coconut, and almonds. Cook 15 minutes longer. Taste for seasoning. Serve with rice.

Serves 6.

MEAT BALL CASSEROLE

1 pound ground beef	2 tablespoons flour
½ pound sausage meat	1½ cups beer
1 egg	½ cup tomato paste
1 teaspoon salt	1 cup sliced stuffed green olives
¼ teaspoon pepper	½ pound broad noodles, cooked
3 tablespoons grated onion	and drained
3 tablespoons salad oil	

Mix together the beef, sausage meat, egg, salt, pepper, and onion. Shape into walnut-size balls. Heat the oil in a skillet and brown the meat balls. Remove and keep warm. Pour off all but 2 tablespoons oil and stir the flour into it, cooking over low heat until browned. Gradually add the beer, stirring constantly to the boiling point. Stir in the tomato paste and then add the meat balls. Cook 5 minutes. Taste for seasoning and add the olives.

Place the noodles in a 2-quart casserole and pour the meat balls and sauce over them. Bake in a 375° oven 20 minutes.

Serves 6.

GLAZED MEAT LOAF

1 pound sausage meat	1 cup beer
1 pound ground ham	1½ teaspoons salt
¼ cup cracker meal	½ teaspoon freshly ground black
3 tablespoons grated onion	pepper
2 tablespoons minced green	¼ teaspoon nutmeg
pepper	¼ teaspoon thyme
1 tablespoon minced parsley	1 cup brown sugar
1 egg yolk	2 teaspoons prepared mustard

Mix together the sausage meat, ham, cracker meal, onion, green pepper, parsley, egg yolk, ¾ cup beer, salt, pepper, nutmeg, and thyme. Shape into a loaf and place on a greased baking pan. Bake in a 350° oven 1 hour.

While the loaf is baking, dissolve the brown sugar in the remaining beer. Stir in the mustard and bring to a boil; let boil vigorously 2 minutes. Pour the mixture over the loaf. Continue baking, basting frequently until top is glazed. Serve hot or cold.

Serves 6–8.

CÔTE DE VEAU À L'OIGNON

1½ cups finely chopped onions	1 teaspoon salt
3 tablespoons butter	¼ teaspoon freshly ground black
¼ cup beer	pepper
1 cup beef broth	½ cup grated Parmesan cheese
4 veal cutlets (about 1 pound)	½ cup dry bread crumbs

Sauté the onions in the butter for 15 minutes over very low heat; stir frequently. Add the beer and ¼ cup of the broth. Season the veal with the salt and pepper, then dip in cheese. Pound in the cheese with a knife or cleaver. Dip the veal lightly in the bread crumbs.

Butter a baking dish and sprinkle some bread crumbs on the bottom. Arrange the cutlets over them and spread the onions over all. Pour a little broth in the dish.

Bake in a 300° oven 1¼ hours, adding more broth as pan becomes dry.

Serves 4.

VIENNA HAMBURGERS

1 pound ground beef	⅛ teaspoon garlic powder
½ cup dry bread crumbs	2 tablespoons grated onion
1½ teaspoons salt	½ cup beer
⅛ teaspoon pepper	

Mix all the ingredients together lightly. Shape into 6 or 8 patties. Broil or pan-fry.

HAMBURGERS IN BEER SAUCE

1½ pounds ground beef   ½ cup beer
2 teaspoons salt   ½ cup chili sauce
¼ teaspoon pepper   1 teaspoon Worcestershire sauce
3 tablespoons water   1 teaspoon sugar
1 tablespoon butter   ⅛ teaspoon Tabasco sauce

Lightly mix together the beef, 1 teaspoon salt, the pepper and water. Shape into 6 or 8 patties. Heat the butter in a skillet; brown the patties on both sides. Mix together the beer, remaining salt, chili sauce, Worcestershire sauce, sugar, and Tabasco; pour over the hamburgers. Cook over high heat 5 minutes, or to desired degree of rareness.

Note: Small meat balls prepared in the same way make excellent hors d'oeuvre.

BAKED MEAT AND MACARONI CASSEROLE

4 tablespoons olive oil   ½ pound elbow macaroni,
½ cup minced onions   cooked and drained
1 pound ground beef   2 tablespoons butter
1 tomato, peeled and chopped   2 tablespoons flour
1½ teaspoons salt   ½ cup beer
½ teaspoon pepper   ½ cup milk
1 cup grated American cheese   1 egg, beaten

Heat the oil in a skillet; add the onions and meat. Cook over high heat, stirring almost constantly for 3 minutes. Add the tomato, salt, and pepper. Cook over low heat 5 minutes. Stir in ½ cup cheese.

Spread half the macaroni on the bottom of a buttered casserole, then turn the meat mixture into it. Cover with the remaining macaroni.

Melt the butter in a saucepan, stir in the flour, then gradually the beer and milk. Cook over low heat, stirring constantly to the boiling point. Mix the remaining cheese with the egg and gradually add to the sauce, stirring constantly. Taste for seasoning. Pour over the macaroni. Bake in a 375° oven 35 minutes, or until browned. Serves 6.

LAMB CHOPS FLAMANDE

½ pound sausage meat
6 loin lamb or mutton chops, 1 inch thick
2 teaspoons salt
½ teaspoon pepper
2 oranges, peeled and sliced thin
1 cup beer

Divide sausage in 6. Wrap the end of each chop around a portion of sausage and fasten with a toothpick; season with the salt and pepper and brown quickly on both sides. Arrange the orange slices in a baking dish with the chops over them. Pour the beer over all; cover. Bake in a 375° oven 1 hour, or until chops are tender. Remove the cover for the last 10 minutes. Serves 6.

LAMB KEBABS

½ cup beer
½ cup pineapple juice
2 tablespoons soy sauce
1 clove garlic, minced
2 pounds boneless lamb, cubed
2 tablespoons salad oil
Green pepper slices, onion slices and tomato wedges

Mix together the beer, pineapple juice, soy sauce, and garlic. Marinate the lamb in this mixture overnight or for at least 4 hours. Drain. On 6 skewers, arrange the meat alternately with the pepper, onion and tomato. Brush the lamb with the oil.

Broil in a hot broiler 10 minutes, turning the skewers frequently. Particularly good when broiled over a charcoal fire. Serve with rice. Serves 6.

VEAL, SEVILLE STYLE

4 veal cutlets (1½ pounds)	2 tablespoons chopped parsley
3 teaspoons salt	3 tablespoons butter
½ teaspoon pepper	3 tablespoons flour
4 tablespoons olive oil	1 cup milk
4 slices ham	½ cup beer
¼ pound mushrooms, chopped	⅛ teaspoon saffron
4 tablespoons minced onions	½ cup blanched sliced almonds

Season the cutlets with half the salt and pepper, and brown in half the oil. Arrange the chops in a casserole or baking dish. Sauté the ham for 2 minutes on each side and place over the cutlets. Sauté the mushrooms, onions, and parsley in the remaining oil for 5 minutes; spread over the ham.

Melt the butter in a saucepan; stir in the flour, then gradually add the milk, stirring constantly to the boiling point. Add the beer, saffron, remaining salt and pepper. Cook over low heat 5 minutes. Pour over the mushrooms and sprinkle with the almonds. Bake in a 350° oven 25 minutes, or until delicately browned.

Serves 4.

VEAL WITH RAREBIT SAUCE

1½ pounds round or loin of veal	4 tablespoons butter
¼ cup flour	1 cup grated Cheddar cheese
1½ teaspoons salt	½ cup beer
¼ teaspoon freshly ground	2 egg yolks, beaten
black pepper	1 tablespoon heavy cream

Have the veal cut very thin and into serving-size pieces. Dip lightly in a mixture of flour, salt, and pepper.

Melt the butter in a skillet and sauté the veal until browned on both sides.

Meanwhile melt the cheese in the top of a double boiler; stir in the beer and then the egg yolks and cream. Cook over low heat, stirring steadily until thick.

Arrange the veal in a baking dish and pour the cheese sauce over it. Place under a hot broiler until browned.

Serves 4–6.

ROLLED VEAL

Breast of veal (about 3 pounds)	¾ cup diced onions
2 tablespoons flour	1½ cups beer
2 teaspoons salt	1 bay leaf
¼ teaspoon pepper	Dash nutmeg
3 tablespoons butter	

Have the veal boned, rolled, and tied. Rub the meat with the flour seasoned with salt and pepper.

Melt the butter in a roasting pan and place the veal in it. Roast in a 425° oven 45 minutes, or until browned. Add the onions, beer, bay leaf, and nutmeg. Reduce heat to 350° and roast 2 hours longer, or until meat is tender. Baste frequently. Discard bay leaf.

Serves 6.

ROAST LOIN OF VEAL

5 pounds loin of veal	¼ teaspoon thyme
2 teaspoons salt	6 sprigs parsley
½ teaspoon pepper	2 stalks celery
3 tablespoons fat	2 cloves
4 carrots, quartered	3 cups beer
3 onions, sliced	1 tablespoon flour
2 cloves garlic, minced	
1 bay leaf	

Have the veal larded. Rub in the salt and pepper. Heat the fat in a shallow roasting pan and brown the meat very well on all sides. Pour off the fat and add the carrots, onions, garlic, bay leaf, thyme, parsley, celery, cloves, and 2 cups of beer. Roast in a 350° oven 2½ hours, or until tender, basting frequently, adding the remaining beer when needed.

Place the roast on a platter and keep warm. Force the gravy and vegetables through a sieve. Mix the flour with a little water and add to the sauce. Cook over low heat, stirring constantly to the boiling point. Taste for seasoning and cook 5 minutes longer. Serves 8–10.

ROAST LEG OF LAMB, DANISH STYLE

1 5- to 6-pound leg of lamb	1 onion, sliced
2 cloves garlic, minced	1 carrot, sliced
1 tablespoon salt	1 bay leaf
½ teaspoon freshly ground black pepper	1½ cups beer

Have the butcher remove the fell (outer skin) of the lamb. Make a paste of the garlic, salt, and pepper; rub into the lamb. Place in a shallow roasting pan and roast in a 450° oven for 30 minutes. Pour off the fat. Add the onion, carrot, bay leaf, and beer. Reduce the heat to 350° and roast 20 minutes per pound, basting frequently. Strain the gravy and serve with the meat. Serves 8–10.

IRISH STEW WITH ALE

½ cup flour	3 tablespoons butter
2 teaspoons salt	3 cups ale
½ teaspoon freshly ground black pepper	1 bay leaf
3 pounds boneless lamb cut in 2-inch cubes	12 small white onions
½ cup diced onions	6 carrots, pared and quartered
	6 potatoes, pared and halved

Mix the flour, salt, and pepper together; roll the lamb in the mixture. Brown the lamb and diced onions in the butter, then add the ale and bay leaf. Cover and cook over low heat 1½ hours. Add the white onions, carrots, and potatoes. Cover and cook over low heat 40 minutes. Taste for seasoning. Discard bay leaf.

Serves 6–8.

SPICED PORK BUTT

1 pork butt (2½ pounds)	2 tablespoons brown sugar
2 cloves	1½ cups beer
1 onion	2 cups water
1 bay leaf	

Place the pork butt in a saucepan with water to cover; bring to a boil and cook 30 minutes. Drain. Stick the cloves in the onion and add to the pork butt with the bay leaf, brown sugar, beer, and water. Bring to a boil; cover loosely and cook over low heat 45 minutes. Drain.

Bake the butt in a shallow roasting pan in a 475° oven until browned, turning it frequently. Serve hot or cold.

Serves 4–6.

ROAST FRESH HAM

½ fresh ham (5–6 pounds)	1 teaspoon paprika
1 tablespoon salt	½ teaspoon savory
¾ teaspoon freshly ground black pepper	2 cloves garlic, minced
	3 cups beer

Buy either end of the ham (or if you use a whole one, double the seasoning). Make a paste of the salt, pepper, paprika, savory, and garlic. Rub the mixture into the meat. Loosen the meat around the bone and force some seasoning in it. If possible, season the day before it is to be roasted.

Place in a shallow roasting pan and roast in a 325° oven 50 minutes a pound. (If thermometer is used, roast until it reads 185°.) Pour off the fat after ¾ hour and add 1 cup beer. Baste frequently and keep adding beer as it evaporates. Delicious hot or cold. Serves 8–10.

GERMAN BREADED PORK

2 pork fillets (about 2½   1½ teaspoons salt
   pounds)   ¼ teaspoon pepper
1 onion   1 cup beer
1 bay leaf   2 egg yolks, beaten
½ teaspoon basil   1½ cups bread crumbs

Combine the fillets, onion, bay leaf, basil, salt, pepper, and beer in a saucepan. Cover and cook over low heat 45 minutes. Remove the fillets and let cool slightly. Reserve the stock.

Dip the pork in the egg yolks and then in the bread crumbs, coating the meat heavily. Place in a shallow baking pan.

Bake in a 400° oven 20 minutes, basting frequently with the stock. Slice crosswise.

Serves 4–6.

PORK AND SAUERKRAUT CASSEROLE

2 pounds sauerkraut   2 cloves garlic, minced
4 cups beer   1½ cups chopped apple
6 pork chops   1½ cups grated potato
1½ teaspoons salt
1 teaspoon freshly ground
   black pepper

Wash the sauerkraut; drain and combine in a saucepan with 2 cups beer. Cook over low heat 2 hours, stirring frequently.

Brown the pork chops on both sides and season with salt and ½ teaspoon pepper. Spread half the sauerkraut on the bottom of a casserole and sprinkle with the remaining pepper and the garlic; arrange the chops over the sauerkraut. Spread the apples and potatoes over them and cover with the sauerkraut. Add the remaining beer. Cover and bake in 350° oven 45 minutes. Remove the cover and bake 15 minutes longer, or until the chops are tender. Serves 6.

GLAZED HAM

Buy the type and size ham you like. Cook it, if necessary, and drain it well. Place the ham in a roasting pan and bake in a 350° oven 45 minutes for a half ham, 1 hour for a whole ham. Baste with 1 cup beer. Remove the ham from the oven and score the fat diagonally in a crisscross pattern. Brush the ham with either of the following:

1¼ cups brown sugar	1 teaspoon dry mustard
3 tablespoons bread crumbs	½ cup beer

Mix the sugar, bread crumbs, and mustard; add enough beer to make a paste.

1 cup applesauce	¼ teaspoon nutmeg
⅔ cup brown sugar	½ cup beer
½ teaspoon cinnamon	

Mix all the ingredients together and spread over the ham.

In either case, stud the ham with cloves and bake 30 minutes longer. Baste occasionally if the bread-crumb mixture is used.

A canned ham may be prepared in the same way, but first cut it in ½-inch slices. Reassemble and tie it with white string. Spread either of the glazes over it and proceed as directed.

PORK BALLS, BELGIAN STYLE

½ cup minced onions	3 egg whites, stiffly beaten
6 tablespoons butter	½ cup cornstarch
6 slices white bread	18 small white onions
1 cup milk	2 cups beer
2 pounds ground pork	1 bay leaf
2 teaspoons salt	½ teaspoon thyme
½ teaspoon pepper	1 clove garlic, minced
¼ teaspoon nutmeg	4 potatoes, peeled and cubed
3 egg yolks	3 tablespoons minced parsley

Sauté the minced onions in 2 tablespoons butter for 10 minutes. Soak the bread in the milk; drain and mash. Mix together the pork, salt, pepper, nutmeg, egg yolks, sautéed onion, and soaked bread. Fold in the egg whites. Shape into 1-inch balls and roll in the cornstarch. Brown the balls in the remaining butter; add the white onions and continue browning. Add the beer, bay leaf, thyme, and garlic. Cover and cook over low heat 15 minutes. Add the potatoes and parsley and cook 15 minutes longer. Taste for seasoning, adding salt and pepper if necessary.
Serves 6–8.

Note: For hot hors d'oeuvre, form teaspoons of the meat into small balls and then roll in equal parts of cornstarch and sesame seeds. Proceed as directed.

BARBECUED SPARERIBS

3 racks spareribs, 6–7 pounds	2½ teaspoons salt
3 cups beer	1½ teaspoons dry mustard
1 cup honey	2 teaspoons ground ginger
2 tablespoons lemon juice	½ teaspoon nutmeg

Have the butcher cut the ribs into serving-size pieces.
Mix the beer, honey, lemon juice, salt, mustard, ginger, and nut-

meg in a deep bowl. Marinate the ribs for 3 hours, turning them and basting frequently. Arrange the ribs in a shallow pan (reserving the marinade). Roast in a 425° oven 15 minutes. Drain the fat and pour 2 cups marinade over the ribs. Reduce heat to 350° and roast 45 minutes longer, basting frequently. Serve with boiled potatoes.

Serves 6–8.

*   *   *

I would give all my fame for a
pot of ale and safety.
                        Shakespeare, Henry V

*   *   *

DEVILED PIGS' FEET

6 pigs' feet	3 tablespoons vinegar
2 onions	6 cloves
2 cloves garlic	2 tablespoons dry mustard
2 teaspoons salt	¼ cup olive or salad oil
½ teaspoon pepper	½ cup bread crumbs
2 bay leaves	½ cup beer

Buy very young, tender pigs' feet. Have them split in half lengthwise. Pour boiling water over them and scrape thoroughly.

In a deep kettle combine the feet, onions, garlic, salt, pepper, bay leaves, vinegar, and cloves with water to cover. Bring to a boil; cover loosely and cook over medium heat 3 hours, or until tender. Drain.

Arrange the feet in a shallow baking pan, cut side down. Mix together the mustard, oil, bread crumbs, and beer, adding just enough to make a spreadable mixture. Spread on the feet.

Broil 5 inches away from heat until browned and crisp.

Sauerkraut, pickles, mashed potatoes, and beer are ideal accompaniments.

Serves 6.

FRANKFURTER RAGOUT

1 tablespoon salad oil	2 cups beer
1 cup diced onions	12 frankfurters cut in 2-inch
2 tablespoons flour	lengths

Heat the oil in a saucepan; sauté the onions for 10 minutes. Sprinkle with flour, stirring until browned. Add the beer and cook over low heat 20 minutes. Add the frankfurters and cook 20 minutes longer.

Delicious with red kidney beans or mashed potatoes. Serves 6.

CHOUCROUTE GARNI

1 slice bacon, chopped	1 whole onion
1 cup diced onions	1 bay leaf
6 slices smoked pork butt	½ teaspoon freshly ground
1½ pounds fresh pork cut in	black pepper
2-inch cubes	1½ cups beer
6 spicy pork sausages	2 cups beef stock
3 pounds sauerkraut, drained	6 frankfurters
3 cloves	

Any combination of pork products and sausages may be used, but the greater the variety the better the dish.

Cook the bacon and onions until lightly browned and transfer to a casserole or Dutch oven. Brown the pork butt and fresh pork; drain. Brown the sausages and drain. Spread the sauerkraut over the browned onions. Arrange the browned meats on top. Stick the cloves in the whole onion and add with the bay leaf, pepper, beer, and stock. Cover and cook over low heat 2 hours. Shake the casserole occasionally to prevent sticking. Add the frankfurters and cook 20 minutes longer, uncovered. Discard bay leaf and onion. Serve directly from the casserole or arrange the sauerkraut with the meat

around it on a heated platter. Boiled potatoes, hot mustard, and lots
of beer are excellent accompaniments.

Serves 8.

FRANKFURTER CASSEROLE

2 pounds sauerkraut   12 beef frankfurters
2 cups beer

Wash and drain the sauerkraut. Combine the sauerkraut and
beer in a casserole; cover and bake in a 350° oven 1½ hours. Arrange the frankfurters on top and bake 20 minutes, uncovered.
Serve directly from the casserole.

Serves 6–12.

MEAT AND BEAN CASSEROLE

3 onions, sliced   ¾ cup beer
2 tablespoons salad oil   1 tablespoon brown sugar
1½ cups diced cooked beef   ½ teaspoon Worcestershire
  or ham   sauce
1 can kidney beans
¾ cup canned, drained
  tomatoes

Sauté the onions in oil for 10 minutes, stirring frequently.
Add the meat, beans, tomatoes, beer, sugar, and Worcestershire
sauce. Mix lightly and taste for seasoning. Turn into a casserole;
cover.

Bake in a 350° oven 1¼ hours, removing the cover after 45
minutes. Serve directly from the casserole, on toast or toasted ham-
burger rolls.

Serves 6.

SAUSAGE PUDDING

1½ pounds sausage meat
3 potatoes, peeled and sliced
  thin
3 eggs
1 cup beer
½ cup heavy cream

1½ cups sifted flour
1 teaspoon baking powder
½ teaspoon salt
⅛ teaspoon cayenne pepper
⅛ teaspoon thyme

Form the sausage meat into 18 small flat cakes. Brown on both sides; remove from pan. Brown the potatoes in the fat remaining in the pan; drain. Arrange the potatoes on the bottom of a 2-quart casserole with the sausage cakes over them.

Beat the eggs, beer, and cream together. Sift the flour, baking powder, salt, cayenne pepper, and thyme into the mixture and beat just until smooth. Turn into the casserole.

Bake in a 450° oven 15 minutes; reduce the heat to 350° and bake 20 minutes longer, or until browned. Serve directly from the casserole.

Serves 6.

PORK SAUSAGES IN BEER, BERLIN STYLE
(*Bratwurst in Bier, Berliner Art*)

18 pork sausages
1 tablespoon butter
2 cups thinly sliced onions
2 cups beer

6 peppercorns
1 bay leaf
1½ tablespoons potato flour

Pour boiling water over the sausages; drain and dry. Brown the sausages in butter, then remove them and drain off all but 2 table-spoons of the fat. Sauté the onions in the fat for 10 minutes. Return the sausages and add the beer, peppercorns, and bay leaf. Cover and cook over low heat 20 minutes.

Go spectacular with skewer cookery, such as *Lamb Kebabs* (recipe on page 61).

Mix the potato flour with enough water to make a thin paste and stir into the pan, mixing constantly to the boiling point. Cook 5 minutes longer. Taste for seasoning; discard bay leaf. Serve with fluffy mashed potatoes.

Serves 6.

ROGNONS A LA BIÈRE

1 pair beef kidneys	¼ teaspoon minced garlic
1 tablespoon vinegar	3 cups beer
3 tablespoons flour	1 teaspoon salt
4 tablespoons butter	¼ teaspoon pepper
2 tablespoons minced onion	⅛ teaspoon thyme

Wash the kidneys thoroughly. Cover with cold water and add the vinegar; soak the kidneys for 10 minutes. Drain. Split and remove the white core. Cover with fresh water and bring to a boil. Drain. Cover with water and bring to a boil again. Cook 2 minutes. Drain and remove the skin. Cut into 1-inch cubes and roll them in flour.

Melt the butter in a skillet; sauté the kidneys, onion, and garlic for 5 minutes. Add the beer, salt, pepper, and thyme. Cover and cook over low heat 30 minutes, or until kidneys are tender. Taste for seasoning. Delicious on toast.

Serves 3–4.

SAUSAGES IN BREAD SAUCE

12 pork sausages	1 teaspoon sugar
2 cups beer	½ teaspoon grated lemon rind
½ cup beef consommé	½ cup dry bread crumbs
1 tablespoon vinegar	

Cook the sausages in the beer for 20 minutes. Remove sausages. Cook the beer until reduced to half; skim the fat. Add the consommé, vinegar, sugar, lemon rind, and bread crumbs. Cook over low heat, stirring constantly until thick and smooth. Return sausages to the pan and heat.

Serves 6.

*   *   *

The Greeks had a word for it—that is, for their favorite beverage of beer—zythos.

*   *   *

TONGUE WITH RAISIN SAUCE

4- to 5-pound smoked or pickled tongue	1 cup beer
1 bay leaf	2 tablespoons brown sugar
1 onion	½ cup seedless raisins
1 clove garlic	1½ tablespoons cornstarch
1 tablespoon sugar	¼ cup sliced, blanched almonds
1 tablespoon water	2 teaspoons grated lemon rind

Combine the tongue, bay leaf, onion, and garlic in a deep kettle; add water to cover. Bring to a boil; cover loosely and cook over low heat 3 hours, or until tongue is tender. Drain, reserving 2 cups of the stock. Remove the skin and root of the tongue.

In a saucepan cook the sugar and water until it caramelizes. Stir in the reserved stock, beer, brown sugar, and raisins. Mix the cornstarch in a little water and add, stirring constantly. Bring to a boil and taste for seasoning. Slice the tongue and heat in the sauce. Add almonds and lemon rind just before serving.

Serves 8–10.

SAVORY SAUSAGE STUFFING

4 tablespoons butter	½ teaspoon pepper
½ cup minced onions	⅛ teaspoon dried thyme
¼ cup diced celery	⅛ teaspoon dried tarragon
¼ cup minced parsley	⅛ teaspoon nutmeg
1 clove garlic, minced	½ pound sausage meat
2 cups bread cubes	½ cup beer
2 teaspoons salt	

Melt the butter in a skillet and sauté the onions 5 minutes. Add the celery, parsley, and garlic; sauté 2 minutes longer. Stir in the bread cubes, salt, pepper, thyme, tarragon, nutmeg, and sausage meat. Toss thoroughly and then add the beer. Cook over low heat 10 minutes, stirring frequently.

Use for stuffing pork roast or poultry. Makes about 5 cups stuffing.

VEGETABLES

BAKED BEANS AND MOLASSES

2 cups pea beans or navy beans
½ pound salt pork, sliced
½ cup molasses
3 cups beer

1 teaspoon dry mustard
½ teaspoon onion powder
1½ teaspoons salt

Wash the beans and cover with cold water; let soak overnight. Drain. Add fresh water to cover. Bring to a boil; cover and cook over low heat 1 hour. Drain, reserving the liquid.

On the bottom of an earthenware pot or casserole arrange half the salt pork; add the beans. Mix together the molasses, beer, mustard, onion powder, and salt. Pour over the beans, lifting around the edges to let the liquid run down. Add only enough of the bean water to reach the top of the beans. Arrange remaining salt pork on top. Cover the pot and bake in a 275° oven 6 hours. Every hour or so add enough bean water to replenish the amount absorbed, always maintaining the same level. Remove cover for last hour of baking time.

Serves 6–8.

BRAISED AMSTERDAM CABBAGE

4 pounds of cabbage
3 tablespoons butter
1 teaspoon salt
¼ teaspoon freshly ground
   black pepper

½ teaspoon sugar
1 tablespoon flour
1¼ cups ale

Shred the cabbage coarsely. Melt the butter in a deep skillet; sauté the cabbage 5 minutes, stirring frequently. Sprinkle with the salt, pepper, sugar, and flour, mixing lightly. Add the ale; cover and cook over low heat 10 minutes.

Serves 6.

POTATO FRITTERS

3 cups mashed potatoes	½ teaspoon baking powder
5 egg yolks	1 cup beer
4 tablespoons melted butter	2 tablespoons salad oil
1½ teaspoons salt	1 egg white, stiffly beaten
¼ teaspoon pepper	Fat for deep frying
1¼ cups sifted flour	

Beat together the potatoes, 4 egg yolks, melted butter, salt, and pepper. Shape into 1-inch balls. Chill.

Mix together the flour, baking powder, beer, remaining egg yolk, and oil; fold in the egg white. Dip the potato balls into the batter. Heat the fat to 370° and drop the balls into it without crowding. Drain and keep hot while preparing the remainder.

Makes about 30 fritters.

BATTER-FRIED ONIONS

1 cup sifted flour	2 tablespoons salad oil
1 teaspoon salt	3–4 large Spanish-type onions
⅛ teaspoon pepper	2 egg whites
2 egg yolks	Fat for frying
⅔ cup beer	

Sift the flour, salt, and pepper into a bowl. Beat together the egg yolks, beer, and oil. Add to the flour mixture, stirring only until smooth. Let stand for 1 hour. Slice the onions ⅛ to ¼ inch thick and separate into rings. Beat the egg whites until stiff but not dry;

fold into the batter. Dip the onions into the batter, coating them thoroughly.

Heat the fat (about 2 inches deep) and fry the onions without crowding until browned on both sides. Drain and keep hot while preparing the balance.

Serves 6.

STUFFED PEPPERS

4 green peppers	3 tablespoons melted butter
4 tomatoes, peeled and chopped	1 teaspoon salt
2 tablespoons grated onion	¼ teaspoon pepper
1 cup cooked rice	½ cup beer

Cut a ½-inch piece from the stem end of the peppers and remove the seeds and fibers. Pour boiling water over them and let soak 10 minutes; drain.

Mix together the tomatoes, onion, rice, butter, salt, and pepper. Stuff the peppers. Arrange them upright in a buttered baking dish. Pour the beer around them.

Bake in a 350° oven 40 minutes, basting frequently. Serve as a vegetable or with ham or bacon as a luncheon dish.

Serves 4.

CANDIED SWEET POTATOES

6 sweet potatoes	2 teaspoons grated orange rind
½ cup brown sugar	½ teaspoon salt
½ cup beer	½ teaspoon ground ginger

Cook the sweet potatoes in boiling water until tender but still firm. Cool, peel, and cut in quarters. Arrange in a shallow baking dish.

Combine the brown sugar, beer, orange rind, salt, and ginger in a saucepan. Cook over low heat until sugar melts and is syrupy; stir frequently. Pour over the potatoes.

Bake in a 400° oven 20 minutes, or until browned. Turn the potatoes once.

Serves 6–8.

SWEET POTATO SOUFFLÉ

2 cups mashed sweet potatoes	½ teaspoon salt
½ cup beer	⅛ teaspoon nutmeg
¼ cup heavy cream	2 teaspoons grated orange rind
4 tablespoons melted butter	4 egg whites, stiffly beaten
4 egg yolks	

Preheat oven to 400°.

Beat the sweet potatoes, beer, cream, butter, egg yolks, salt, nutmeg, and orange rind until fluffy. Fold in the egg whites. Turn into a buttered 1½-quart soufflé dish. Bake 25 minutes, or until browned and set. Serve at once.

Serves 6.

CHEESE

CHEESE CUSTARD

4 slices bacon	¾ cup grated Swiss cheese
2 eggs	¼ cup grated Parmesan cheese
½ cup heavy cream	½ teaspoon salt
½ cup beer	¼ teaspoon pepper

Preheat oven to 425°.

Fry the bacon until crisp; drain and crumble.

Beat the eggs, cream, and beer together; stir in the bacon, Swiss cheese, Parmesan cheese, salt, and pepper. Pour into 6 custard cups. Set the cups in a shallow pan of hot water.

Bake 20 minutes, or until a knife inserted in the center comes out clean. Serve at once.

Serves 6.

CHEESE SOUFFLÉ

4 tablespoons butter	½ teaspoon dry mustard
4 tablespoons flour	2 cups (½ pound) grated
1 cup milk	Cheddar cheese
1 cup beer	5 egg yolks
1 teaspoon salt	5 egg whites

Over low heat, melt the butter in a saucepan; stir in the flour until smooth. Gradually add the milk and beer, stirring constantly to the boiling point. Cook over low heat 5 minutes. Stir in the salt, mustard and cheese, mixing until cheese melts.

Beat the egg yolks in a bowl; gradually add the hot mixture, stirring steadily to prevent curdling. Cool 20 minutes. Preheat oven to 375°.

Beat the egg whites until stiff but not dry; fold into the cheese mixture. Pour into a buttered 2-quart soufflé dish. Bake 40 minutes, or until browned and set. Serve at once.

Serves 4–6.

FONDUE PUDDING

4 tablespoons butter	½ teaspoon dry mustard
10 slices white bread, trimmed	⅛ teaspoon freshly ground
10 slices American cheese	black pepper
3 eggs	1½ cups beer
½ teaspoon salt	

Preheat oven to 350°.

Butter the bread. In a buttered casserole arrange layers of the bread and cheese. Beat together the eggs, salt, mustard, and pepper. Stir in the beer; pour over the layers.

Bake 45 minutes, or until set and browned. Sprinkle with crumbled bacon or serve with fried ham if desired.

Serves 6–8.

*   *   *

Gambrinus, always pictured as a jolly, round-faced man, was the mythical Flemish king whom the brewers regarded as the patron of beer. It is said that Gambrinus first learned the recipe for making beer from an angel (with a good memory) in a dream. It has been suggested by historians that the name Gambrinus is a popular corruption of Jan Primus (the First), Duke of Brabant, a man renowned for the quantity of beer he could consume.

QUICHE AU FROMAGE

1 tablespoon flour	¾ cup beer or ale
2 cups (½ pound) Cheddar cheese, grated	¼ cup heavy cream
	½ teaspoon salt
1 9-inch unbaked pie shell	Dash cayenne pepper
4 egg yolks	

Preheat oven to 400°.

Mix the flour and cheese together; turn into the pie shell. Beat the egg yolks, then add the beer, cream, salt, and cayenne pepper. Pour over the cheese.

Bake 40 minutes, or until browned and set. Cut into pie-shaped wedges.

Note: For hot hors d'oeuvre, make 3-inch tarts in the same manner. The amount of cheese and beer mixture is enough for about 24 tarts. Bake 20 minutes, or until set and browned.

FONDUE DANOIS

8 slices white bread	3 cups (¾ pound) grated Cheddar cheese
4 egg yolks	
1¼ cups milk, scalded and cooled	4 egg whites, stiffly beaten
	3 tablespoons melted butter
¾ cup beer	1 tablespoon poppy or caraway seeds
1 teaspoon salt	
½ teaspoon dry mustard	

Preheat oven to 325°.

Trim the bread and cut each slice into 6 pieces.

Beat the egg yolks and stir in the milk, beer, salt, mustard, and cheese. Fold in the egg whites. Add the bread (reserving 8 pieces) and mix lightly. Turn the mixture into a buttered 1½-quart shallow casserole. Toss the remaining bread with the melted butter and arrange on top. Sprinkle with the poppy or caraway seeds.

Bake 1¼ hours, or until a knife inserted in the center comes out clean. Serve at once.
Serves 6–8.

BAVARIAN FONDUE

1½ cups beer	1 teaspoon salt
1 pound Swiss or Gruyère cheese, cubed	¼ teaspoon freshly ground black pepper
1 tablespoon potato flour or cornstarch	⅛ teaspoon nutmeg
2 tablespoons water	French bread

Use a chafing dish (with hot water underneath) or a double boiler. Heat the beer to the boiling point over hot water. Add the cheese a little at a time, stirring until it melts. Mix the potato flour, water, salt, pepper, and nutmeg until smooth. Stir into the cheese mixture. Cook, stirring constantly, until thickened.

Cut the bread into bite-size pieces, and supply forks for spearing. Each person dips the bread into the fondue.
Serves 4–6.

PARMESAN CHEESE SOUFFLÉ

4 tablespoons butter	Dash cayenne pepper
⅓ cup flour	5 egg yolks
1 cup light cream	1¼ cups grated Parmesan cheese
1 cup beer	5 egg whites
½ teaspoon salt	

Melt the butter in a saucepan; stir in the flour. Gradually add the cream and beer, stirring constantly to the boiling point. Add the salt and cayenne pepper. Cook over low heat 5 minutes.

Beat the egg yolks in a bowl; gradually add the hot sauce, stirring steadily to prevent curdling. Blend in the cheese. Cool 15 minutes. Preheat oven to 375°.

Beat the egg whites until stiff but not dry; fold into the cheese mixture. Pour into a 2-quart soufflé dish or casserole. Bake 35 minutes, or until browned, puffy, and set. Serve at once.

Serves 4–6.

Whether you call it Rarebit or Rabbit, it's still the same dish, and all delicious.

WELSH RAREBIT

2 tablespoons butter	2 teaspoons dry mustard
4 cups (1 pound) grated Cheddar or Swiss cheese	1 teaspoon Worcestershire sauce
¾ cup beer	1 egg
½ teaspoon salt	

In the top of a double boiler or chafing dish, melt the butter. Place over hot water and add the cheese; let melt. Mix the beer with the salt, mustard, and Worcestershire sauce; gradually add to the cheese, stirring constantly until smooth.

Beat the egg yolk; add a little of the cheese mixture, stirring constantly to prevent curdling. Return to balance of cheese mixture, mixing steadily. Serve on buttered toast.   Serves 4–6.

BUCK RAREBIT

Place a lightly poached egg on top of the Welsh Rarebit for each serving.

TOMATO RAREBIT

1 can (10½ ounces) condensed tomato soup	3 cups grated American cheese
⅔ cup beer	½ teaspoon dry mustard

Mix the soup and beer until very smooth; stir in the cheese and mustard. Cook over low heat, stirring frequently until cheese melts. Delicious on toasted English muffins.

Serves 4–6.

WELSH RAREBIT WITH OYSTERS

3 tablespoons butter	1 teaspoon dry mustard
3 cups (¾ pound) grated American cheese	½ teaspoon paprika
	1 cup beer
1 teaspoon salt	24 small oysters, shucked

In a saucepan or chafing dish, combine the butter, cheese, salt, mustard, and paprika. Cook over low heat, stirring constantly until cheese begins to melt. Gradually add the beer and continue stirring constantly until almost smooth. Add the oysters; cook 3 minutes. Serve on toast.

Serves 6.

BAKED RAREBIT

2 egg yolks	Dash cayenne pepper
½ cup heavy cream	½ teaspoon dry mustard
2 tablespoons melted butter	2 cups grated Cheddar cheese
½ teaspoon salt	½ cup ale or beer

Preheat oven to 375°.

Beat the egg yolks, cream, butter, salt, cayenne pepper, and mustard together. Stir in the cheese and then the ale or beer. Turn into a buttered 1-quart baking dish. Bake 25 minutes.

Serve with toast points or English muffins.

Serves 4.

CHEESE-RICE CROQUETTES

4 tablespoons butter	½ cup milk
4 tablespoons flour	1 cup grated Cheddar cheese
¾ teaspoon salt	1½ cups cooked rice
⅛ teaspoon pepper	¾ cup dry bread crumbs
¼ teaspoon dry mustard	1 egg, beaten
½ cup beer	Fat for deep frying

Melt the butter; stir in the flour, salt, pepper, and mustard. Gradually add the beer and milk, stirring constantly to the boiling point. Add cheese and cook until it melts. Stir in the rice. Spread mixture in a shallow pan and chill.

Form into 12 croquettes. Roll croquettes first in the crumbs, then the egg, and again in the crumbs.

Fry in 375° fat until browned. Drain.

Serves 6–12.

GOLDEN BUCK

2 cups diced sharp Cheddar cheese	1 teaspoon lemon juice
1 cup ale or beer	4 egg yolks, beaten
1 teaspoon Worcestershire sauce	

Use a chafing dish or top of a double boiler. Have the water under it simmering and barely touching.

Combine the cheese, ale, Worcestershire sauce, and lemon juice in the chafing dish or top of double boiler. Cook, stirring constantly, until melted and smooth. Still mixing steadily, add the egg yolks and cook until mixture thickens.

Serve immediately on buttered toast or English muffins. If you like, spread the toast or muffins with anchovy paste.

Serves 4.

NOODLE-CHEESE PUDDING

3 eggs	1 cup cottage cheese
¾ cup beer	½ pound fine noodles, half
1¼ teaspoons salt	cooked and drained
¼ teaspoon white pepper	4 tablespoons melted butter
1½ cups grated Cheddar cheese	

Preheat oven to 325°.

Beat together the eggs, beer, salt, and pepper. Add the Cheddar cheese, cottage cheese, noodles, and butter, tossing until well blended. Turn into a buttered 2-quart casserole. Bake 45 minutes, or until browned. Serve hot, from the casserole.

Serves 6.

DRESSINGS AND SAUCES

BEER DRESSING (*for Potato Salad*)

½ cup diced onions
3 tablespoons salad oil
2 tablespoons flour
1½ teaspoons salt

⅛ teaspoon pepper
2 teaspoons sugar
1½ cups beer
¼ cup cider vinegar

Sauté the onions in oil for 10 minutes, stirring frequently. Blend in the flour, salt, pepper and sugar. Gradually add the beer and vinegar, stirring constantly to the boiling point. Cook over low heat 5 minutes.

Cool slightly and pour over the potatoes.

Makes about 1¾ cups.

ORIENTAL BARBECUE SAUCE

1½ cups beer
½ teaspoon salt
1 tablespoon dry mustard
1 teaspoon ground ginger
3 tablespoons soy sauce

⅛ teaspoon Tabasco sauce
2 tablespoons sugar
4 tablespoons orange
   marmalade
2 cloves garlic, minced

Combine all the ingredients in a bowl. Use as a marinade for pork, spareribs, lamb ribs, chicken, or ham before roasting or broiling the meat.

Makes about 2 cups.

BOILED DRESSING

3 tablespoons cornstarch	1 teaspoon dry mustard
1¼ cups milk	1 tablespoon butter
1 teaspoon salt	½ cup beer

Mix the cornstarch and milk in the top of a double boiler. Place over hot water and cook, stirring steadily until mixture thickens. Stir in the salt, mustard, butter, and beer. Cook 10 minutes, stirring frequently. Serve as a dressing for potato salad or coleslaw. Makes about 1½ cups.

SALAD DRESSING

½ cup olive oil	⅛ teaspoon freshly ground
3 tablespoons wine vinegar	black pepper
¼ cup beer	Dash garlic powder
¾ teaspoon salt	

Beat or shake all the ingredients together. Delicious with potato salad, coleslaw, meat salads. Makes about 1 cup.

BARBECUE SAUCE

1 cup beer	2 teaspoons sugar
1½ cups chili sauce	2 tablespoons Worcestershire
2 tablespoons grated onion	sauce
2 tablespoons vinegar	2 teaspoons chili powder

Combine all the ingredients in a saucepan; bring to a boil and cook 2 minutes. Delicious as a basting sauce for chicken, spareribs, or frankfurters. Makes about 3 cups.

MAYONNAISE DRESSING

½ cup beer   1 cup mayonnaise

Gradually add the beer to the mayonnaise. Serve on coleslaw, with cold cuts.

Makes about 1½ cups.

*   *   *

A sturdy tribe, the Saxons, whose home was at the mouth of the river Elbe in what is today Germany, were fond of raiding southeastern Britain. Together with a friendly tribe, the Angles, they eventually took over a large section of the coast line and later established the kingdom of the West Saxons, called Wessex, during the sixth century. Hearty drinkers, the Saxons liked ale and beer in enormous quantities. Since drinking containers were scarce, most inns only had one or two. It became customary to mark the interior of the tankards with wooden pegs, and each Saxon drank to the next peg. Even today the British offer a guest a drink with the expression, "Have a peg."

CHEESE SAUCE

2 cups grated Cheddar cheese   ½ teaspoon salt
1 tablespoon butter   ½ teaspoon dry mustard
½ cup ale or beer   Dash cayenne pepper
1 teaspoon Worcestershire
sauce

Combine the cheese and butter in the top of a double boiler. Place over hot water until cheese begins to melt. Gradually add the ale or beer, stirring until smooth. Stir in the Worcestershire sauce, salt, mustard and cayenne pepper.

Delicious with asparagus, broccoli, or hard-cooked eggs.

Makes about 2½ cups.

MUSHROOM STEAK SAUCE

4 tablespoons butter   ¾ teaspoon salt
1 onion, minced   2 tablespoons flour
½ pound mushrooms, sliced   1½ cups beer

Melt the butter in a skillet; sauté the onion and mushrooms 10 minutes. Sprinkle with salt and flour; gradually add the beer, stirring constantly to the boiling point. Cook over low heat 5 minutes longer.

Serve with steak or chops.

Makes about 1¾ cups.

BEER-MUSHROOM SAUCE

3 tablespoons butter   ½ teaspoon salt
2 tablespoons minced onion   Dash cayenne pepper
½ pound mushrooms, sliced   2 cups beer
2 tablespoons flour

Melt the butter in a skillet; sauté the onion 2 minutes. Add the mushrooms and cook 3 minutes. Sprinkle with flour, salt and pepper; stir in the beer. Cook over low heat 10 minutes, stirring frequently. Delicious with steak and hamburgers.

Makes about 2½ cups.

ORANGE GAME SAUCE

3 tablespoons grated orange rind
1 tablespoon cornstarch
1 cup orange juice

½ cup chicken consommé
½ cup ale or beer
1 tablespoon brown sugar
½ teaspoon salt

Pour boiling water over the rind and let it soak for 10 minutes. Drain.

Mix the cornstarch with a little orange juice until smooth. Combine in a saucepan with the remaining orange juice, the consommé, beer, brown sugar, and salt. Cook over low heat, stirring constantly, to the boiling point. Add the rind and cook 10 minutes more. Serve with game or duck.

Makes about 1½ cups.

ORANGE DESSERT SAUCE

½ cup beer
½ cup orange juice
1 tablespoon grated orange rind

½ cup brown sugar
2 tablespoons butter

Combine all the ingredients in a saucepan and cook, stirring occasionally, until mixture is syrupy. Serve on plain cakes, pancakes, or ice cream.

Makes about 1¼ cups.

BEER HARD SAUCE

¼ pound sweet butter   3 tablespoons beer
¼ cup sugar

Cream together the butter and sugar; blend in the beer. Chill.
Serve with mince or apple pie or plum pudding.
Makes ⅔ cup.

This is a classic New England recipe, which originated in the
earliest days of the Pilgrims.

PILGRIM'S SYRUP

1 cup beer
1 cup brown sugar

Cook the beer and brown sugar over low heat for 15 minutes,
or until syrupy. Serve warm or cold with pancakes, French toast,
or waffles.
Makes about 1½ cups.

EGGS

RAREBIT OMELET

4 eggs
¼ cup beer
½ teaspoon salt

⅛ teaspoon Tabasco
2 tablespoons butter
⅓ cup grated Cheddar cheese

Beat together the eggs, beer, salt, and Tabasco sauce until blended but not frothy.

In an 8-inch skillet, melt 1 tablespoon of butter until it sizzles. Pour half of the egg mixture into the skillet. Holding the handle with one hand, move the pan back and forth, while with the other mix the eggs gently with a fork until the bottom is set. Sprinkle with half the cheese. Tip the pan, gently fold the omelet, and roll it out onto a heated dish. Repeat with the balance.

Serves 2.

OEUFS A L'ALSACE

1½ cups beer
2 cups grated Swiss cheese
3 tablespoons butter
2 teaspoons minced onion
2 teaspoons minced parsley
¾ teaspoon salt

½ teaspoon freshly ground
   black pepper
⅛ teaspoon nutmeg
6 egg yolks, beaten
6 egg whites, stiffly beaten

Use a heatproof casserole (not aluminum). In the casserole, combine the beer, Swiss cheese, butter, onion, parsley, salt, pepper, and nutmeg. Cook over low heat, stirring constantly until the cheese melts and boils. Very gradually add the egg yolks, then the egg whites, beating steadily and scraping the bottom, until the mixture has the consistency of scrambled eggs. Serve on toast and garnish with an anchovy if desired.

Serves 6.

OMELET SOUFFLÉ

2 egg whites	2 egg yolks
¼ teaspoon salt	2 tablespoons beer
Dash white pepper	2 tablespoons butter

Beat the egg whites, salt, and pepper until stiff but not dry. Beat the egg yolks and beer until frothy; fold into the egg whites.

Melt the butter in a 7-inch skillet and cook egg mixture over low heat until the underside is browned and omelet is puffed. Lift edges as omelet cooks to permit the unset part to run under. Place under a hot broiler for a few seconds to set the top. Carefully slide out onto a heated plate and fold in half.

Serves 1.

Note: You may vary the omelet by adding to the egg yolks one of the following:

1 tablespoon chopped chives or onions
½ teaspoon dried herbs
3 tablespoons grated Parmesan cheese

*   *   *

When the future King Fredrick the Great was a boy in his teens, he served as a brewer's apprentice for about a year; it was regarded as part of his necessary preparation before reaching the throne.

BAVARIAN EGG PIE

4 firm tomatoes	6 eggs
3 tablespoons minced onions	1½ teaspoons salt
2 tablespoons parsley	¼ teaspoon white pepper
6 hard-cooked eggs, sliced	1 cup heavy cream
½ cup dry bread crumbs	½ cup beer
2 tablespoons butter	

Preheat oven to 350°.

Slice the tomatoes 1 inch thick and arrange on the bottom of a buttered, deep 9-inch pie plate. Sprinkle with the onions and parsley. Arrange layers of the sliced egg and bread crumbs dotted with butter.

Beat together the eggs, salt, pepper, cream, and beer and pour carefully over the top. Bake 40 minutes, or until a knife inserted in the center comes out clean.

Serves 4–6.

BAKED ALSATIAN EGGS

½ cup chopped green pepper	¼ teaspoon freshly ground
½ cup minced onion	black pepper
¼ teaspoon minced garlic	¼ cup grated Cheddar cheese
4 tablespoons butter	3 tablespoons dry bread
4 eggs	crumbs
¾ teaspoon salt	½ cup beer

Preheat oven to 375°.

Sauté the green pepper, onion, and garlic in 3 tablespoons butter for 10 minutes, stirring occasionally. Spread over the bottom of 2 ramekins or baking dishes. Carefully break 2 eggs into each dish; sprinkle with salt, pepper, cheese, and bread crumbs. Pour the beer over all and dot with remaining butter.

Bake 10 minutes, or until eggs are set.

Serves 2.

BREADS AND PANCAKES

BAKING POWDER BRIOCHE

2 cups sifted flour	4 eggs
½ teaspoon salt	⅓ cup beer
⅓ cup sugar	¾ cup (6 ounces) butter,
1 tablespoon baking powder	softened

Sift together the flour, salt, sugar, and baking powder. Beat the eggs until light and fluffy. Alternately add the flour mixture and the beer. Beat in the butter. Cover and let stand in a cool place (not the refrigerator) overnight. (The batter may be baked after 1 hour, but the longer time improves the flavor.) Preheat oven to 375°.

Bake in 24 buttered muffin tins 15 minutes or in a 10-inch loaf pan 35 minutes, or until browned.

The beer supplies the flavor and lightness of yeast, without the trouble of kneading and rising.

CHEESE BRIOCHE (*Gannat*)

1 cake or package yeast	3 egg yolks
⅓ cup lukewarm water	¼ pound butter, softened
2 cups sifted flour	¼ cup beer
½ teaspoon salt	¾ cup diced Swiss cheese
3 eggs	

Soften the yeast in water for 5 minutes. Sift ¾ cup flour into a small bowl and add the yeast, mixing until a firm dough is formed.

Place the dough in a deep bowl filled with warm water. Let rise until it floats to the top.

Sift the remaining flour and the salt into a bowl. Beat together the eggs and egg yolks; add to the flour with the butter and beer. Work together with the hand until a soft dough is formed, then work in the cheese. Knead egg dough into the yeast dough. Cover and let rise in a warm place until double in bulk. Punch down and turn dough into a buttered 9-inch round pan (2 inches deep). Cover and let rise again until double in bulk. Brush top with beaten egg yolk.

Bake in a 425° oven 40 minutes, or until browned.

SWEDISH LIMPA BREAD

1½ cups ale or beer	¾ cup lukewarm water
2 tablespoons brown sugar	3½ cups sifted white flour
2 tablespoons salad oil	2¼ cups sifted rye flour
3 tablespoons molasses	1 tablespoon salt
¼ teaspoon anise seed	2 teaspoons grated orange rind
1 cake or package yeast	1 teaspoon cornstarch

Bring to a boil 1 cup ale or beer, the brown sugar, oil, molasses, and anise; cook over low heat 5 minutes. Cool.

In a large bowl, soften the yeast in the water. Stir in the beer mixture and the white flour. Beat until smooth. Cover with a towel and let rise in a warm place until double in bulk, about 30 minutes. Work in the rye flour, salt, and orange rind until smooth. Cover and let rise in a warm place until double in bulk, about 45 minutes.

Turn dough out on a lightly floured surface and knead until very smooth. Divide dough in two. You may form the dough into round or long loaves, or make one of each.

For round loaves, tuck the edges under to form a smooth top. Place in well-greased 8-inch pie plates. Cut ¼-inch-deep gashes at regular intervals (about 2–3 inches) around the loaves.

For long loaves, roll each half into rectangles about 12 × 15 inches. Roll up like a jelly roll, sealing the edges well after each turn. Place on well-greased baking sheets. Cut ¼-inch-deep diagonal gashes 2 inches apart.

Mix the cornstarch with remaining beer and cook over low heat until slightly thickened. Cool. Brush tops of loaves with this glaze. Cover with towels and let rise in a warm place until double in bulk, about 45 minutes. Brush again with the glaze.

Bake in a 350° oven 50 minutes, or until browned.

Cool on a cake rack. For a smooth top, keep free of drafts. For a cracked top, cool in a draft.

SOUR RYE BREAD

1 cake or package yeast	1 cup sour milk or buttermilk
1 tablespoon sugar	¾ cup beer
¼ cup lukewarm water	2 teaspoons salt
2 cups sifted white flour	3 tablespoons caraway seeds
5 cups rye flour	(optional)
½ cup whole-wheat flour	

Combine the yeast, sugar, and water; let soften for 5 minutes. Stir in ½ cup white flour; let stand until bubbles form. Add the remaining white flour, rye flour, whole-wheat flour, sour milk, beer, salt, and caraway seeds, mixing until a dough is formed. Knead on a lightly floured surface until smooth and elastic, about 10 minutes.

Put the dough in a floured bowl, cover with a towel, and let rise in a warm place until double in bulk, about 1½ hours. Punch down and form into 2 loaves or 1 loaf and rolls. Place the loaves in buttered pans or the rolls on a buttered baking pan. Cover and let rise again until double in bulk.

Bake in a 400° oven 15 minutes; reduce the heat to 350° and bake 1¼ hours longer, or until browned. The rolls will require about 35 minutes.

DATE-NUT BREAD

1 cup beer	4 tablespoons butter
2 cups chopped dates	¾ cup dark brown sugar,
1¾ cups sifted flour	packed
½ teaspoon salt	2 eggs
1½ teaspoons baking soda	1 cup coarsely chopped walnuts

Preheat oven to 350°. Bring the beer and dates to a boil and let cool.

Sift together the flour, salt, and baking soda. Cream the butter; add the brown sugar and beat until light and fluffy. Beat in the eggs. Alternately add the flour mixture and the beer-date mixture, beating after each addition. Stir in the nuts.

Bake in a 10-inch buttered loaf pan 55 minutes, or until a cake tester comes out clean. Carefully remove the loaf from the pan and let cool on a cake rack. Let stand 24 hours before serving.

*   *   *

Making beer was a matter of luck and incantation during the eighth and ninth centuries; present-day scientific methods were of course unknown. When the brew was successful, the happy innkeeper proclaimed his good fortune to the world by placing ale garlands on the door. These were two small wooden circles with laurel leaves entwined about them and decorated with a sprig of young barley.

HUSH PUPPIES

2 cups yellow corn meal	1 egg
2 teaspoons double-action baking powder	1½ cups milk
	½ cup beer
¾ teaspoon salt	Fat for frying
¼ cup grated onion	

Mix together the corn meal, baking powder, salt, and onion in a bowl. Lightly beat the egg, milk, and beer; stir into the corn-meal mixture. Shape into balls or oblongs.

In a heavy skillet, heat 2 inches of fat. Fry Hush Puppies until browned on both sides. Serve hot with fried fish, ham, or bacon. Serves 6–8.

You may prepare the batter the night before if you like, just as they did in colonial days.

FLAPJACKS

1½ cups sifted flour	2 egg yolks
¾ teaspoon salt	3 tablespoons melted butter
1½ teaspoons double-action baking powder	½ cup beer
	⅔ cup milk
2 teaspoons sugar	1 egg white, stiffly beaten

Sift together the flour, salt, baking powder, and sugar. Beat together the egg yolks, butter, beer, and milk. Add to flour mixture, stirring until smooth. Fold in the egg white.

Drop by the tablespoonful onto a hot greased griddle or skillet. Bake until bubbles cover the top, then turn and bake until browned on other side. Don't turn more than once. Serve with hot Pilgrim's syrup or maple syrup.   Makes about 18 3-inch pancakes.

Note: Use your favorite pancake mix if you prefer and substitute beer for the liquid specified on the package.

HAM FLAPJACKS

Add ¾ cup finely chopped ham to the batter. Proceed as directed.

FRIED BREAKFAST TOAST (*Pain Perdu*)

4 slices white bread	2 egg yolks
1 cup beer	½ cup warm milk
2 tablespoons sugar	3 tablespoons butter

Trim the bread and cut in half. Soak for 5 minutes in a mixture of beer and sugar. Drain. Beat the egg yolks and milk together and dip the bread in the mixture.

Melt the butter in a skillet and fry the bread until browned on both sides. Sprinkle with powdered sugar if desired. Serves 2–4.

*   *   *

Beer supplies a lightness and added tang to ordinary fritter batter. It's an old and delicious cooking technique utilized in the best of European cooking.

FRITTER BATTER

1 cup sifted flour	⅔ cup beer
½ teaspoon salt	2 tablespoons melted butter
2 egg yolks	2 egg whites

Sift the flour and salt into a bowl. Beat the egg yolks and stir in the beer. Add to the flour, stirring only until blended. Add butter and let stand 1 hour.

Beat the egg whites until stiff but not dry and fold into the yolk mixture. Use for seafood, chicken, or vegetables.

YEAST FRITTER BATTER

¾ cup beer
1 teaspoon dry yeast
¼ cup lukewarm water
1 cup flour

⅛ teaspoon salt
1 tablespoon salad oil
1 egg white, stiffly beaten

Heat the beer slightly. Soften the yeast in the water. Combine the flour and salt in a bowl; make a well in the center and drop the yeast into it. Work in the flour and gradually add the beer and oil. Beat for 2 minutes. The batter should have the consistency of thick cream. If not, add a little water. Cover and set aside for 45 minutes in a warm place. Fold in the egg white just before using.

Use for vegetables, meat, fish. For dessert fritters, add 1½ teaspoons sugar. Dip the selected food in the batter and fry in hot deep fat until browned.

DESSERTS

DUTCH APPLE CAKE

1⅓ cups sugar	¾ teaspoon baking powder
¾ cup beer	4 egg yolks
¾ cup water	⅔ cup heavy cream
½ teaspoon cinnamon	2 tablespoons melted butter
8 apples, peeled and quartered	4 egg whites, stiffly beaten
⅔ cup sifted flour	2 tablespoons brown sugar

Combine 1 cup sugar, the beer, water, and cinnamon in a saucepan; bring to a boil and cook over medium heat 5 minutes. Add the apples and cook over low heat until tender but slightly firm. Turn into a 2-quart buttered casserole. Preheat oven to 425°.

Sift together the flour, baking powder, and remaining sugar. Beat the egg yolks until light; add the cream and butter. Gently stir in the flour mixture, then fold in the egg whites. Pour over the apples and sprinkle with brown sugar. Set in a shallow pan of water and bake 30 minutes, or until browned and set.

Serve warm with a foamy sauce.

Serves 6–8.

BEIGNETS

1 cup beer	⅛ teaspoon salt
¼ pound butter	4 eggs
1 cup sifted flour	Fat for deep frying
2 tablespoons sugar	

Cook the beer and butter until butter melts. Mix together the flour, sugar, and salt and add to the beer mixture all at once. Cook over low heat, beating vigorously until mixture leaves the sides of the pan. Remove from heat. Add 1 egg at a time, beating until absorbed after each addition. Chill for 30 minutes.

Drop half teaspoonfuls into 350° fat. Fry, turning frequently until browned. Drain and dust with confectioners' sugar.

Makes about 3 dozen.

APPLE DUMPLINGS

1½ cups sifted flour	6 tablespoons sugar
¼ teaspoon salt	1 teaspoon grated lemon rind
¾ cup shortening	½ cup ale or beer
4 tablespoons ice water	3 cloves
6 tart apples	½ teaspoon cinnamon
3 tablespoons butter	¼ teaspoon nutmeg

Sift the flour and salt into a bowl. Cut in the shortening and add the water, tossing until a ball of dough is formed. Chill 1 hour. Preheat oven to 375°.

Wash, dry, and core the apples. Cream together the butter, sugar, and lemon rind. Fill the centers with the mixture. Roll out the dough as thin as possible and cut into pieces large enough to wrap around the apples. Pinch the edges together, but leave a small opening. Arrange on a baking pan.

Bake 45 minutes. When the baking time is almost up, boil together the ale or beer, cloves, cinnamon, and nutmeg for 5 minutes. Strain. Remove apples from oven and pour mixture into the openings. Serve warm.

Makes 6 dumplings.

* * *

Shoulder the sky, my lad,
and drink your ale.

A. E. *Housman*

APPLE FRITTERS

4 apples, peeled and cored
6 tablespoons sugar
½ teaspoon cinnamon
1 cup sifted flour
¼ teaspoon salt

1 teaspoon baking powder
2 eggs
¾ cup beer
2 tablespoons melted butter
Fat for deep frying

Slice the apples about ¼ inch thick and sprinkle with 3 tablespoons sugar and the cinnamon.

Sift together the flour, salt, baking powder, and remaining sugar. Beat the eggs, beer, and melted butter together. Add to the flour mixture, beating until smooth.

Dip the apple slices in the batter and fry in 370° fat until browned on both sides. Drain. Sprinkle with confectioners' sugar.

Makes about 20 fritters.

BERLIN BEER CAKE

2⅔ cups sifted flour
½ teaspoon salt
1 tablespoon baking powder
¼ teaspoon baking soda
1 teaspoon cinnamon
½ teaspoon nutmeg
¼ teaspoon ginger

¼ pound butter
1 cup molasses
1½ cups beer
1 cup seedless white raisins
1 cup coarsely chopped nuts
(walnuts, filberts)

Preheat oven to 350°. Grease a 9-inch tube pan and dust lightly with flour.

Sift together the flour, salt, baking powder, soda, cinnamon, nutmeg, and ginger. Combine the butter, molasses, and beer in a saucepan; heat until butter melts. Stir in the raisins. Cool 15 minutes. Mix the sifted dry ingredients with the beer mixture, stirring until smooth. Add the nuts.

Bake 1 hour, or until a cake tester comes out clean. Cool on a cake rack. This is a moist, heavy cake which keeps well.

CHIFFON PIE

1 envelope unflavored gelatine
¼ cup water
3 egg yolks
6 tablespoons sugar

1 cup beer
1 cup heavy cream, whipped
8-inch baked pastry or crumb
  shell

Soften the gelatine in the water.

Beat the egg yolks; gradually add the sugar and beer. Place over hot water and cook, stirring constantly until thick. Stir in the gelatine until dissolved. Cool until mixture begins to thicken. Fold in the whipped cream. Pour into the pie shell and decorate with whipped cream and berries, or shaved chocolate.

CHOCOLATE LAYER CAKE

2 squares (ounces) unsweetened chocolate
1⅔ cups sifted flour
¼ teaspoon salt
1½ teaspoons baking powder

¼ teaspoon baking soda
½ cup shortening
1 cup sugar
2 eggs
¾ cup beer

Preheat oven to 350°. Grease 2 8-inch layer-cake pans and dust lightly with flour.

Melt the chocolate over hot water. Cool. Sift together the flour, salt, baking powder, and soda.

Cream the shortening, gradually adding the sugar; beat until light and fluffy. Add 1 egg at a time, beating well after each addition. Stir in the chocolate. Add the flour mixture alternately with the beer, mixing until well blended. Turn into the pans.

Bake 25 minutes, or until a cake tester comes out clean. Cool for 5 minutes in the pans and then turn out onto a cake rack. Let cool completely before frosting. Put layers together with whipped cream or butter frosting.

CREAM TART

⅓ cup sifted flour	1½ cups beer
¾ cup sugar	1 teaspoon vanilla extract
⅛ teaspoon salt	¾ cup heavy cream, whipped
6 egg yolks	Baked 9-inch pastry or
1½ cups milk, scalded	crumb shell

Sift the flour, sugar, and salt into a saucepan; beat in the egg yolks; gradually add the milk and beer, stirring steadily. Cook over low heat, stirring constantly until thick and smooth. Add the vanilla. Cool, stirring occasionally. Fold in the whipped cream and turn into the pie shell.

Sliced bananas, grated chocolate, or nuts are delicious on top of the cream, but it's equally good plain or decorated with whipped cream.

FLUFFY CHEESE PIE

Crust:

24 graham crackers	¼ pound butter, melted
¼ cup sugar	

Crush the graham crackers until very fine; blend in the sugar and butter. Press against the sides and bottom of a greased 9-inch pie plate. Chill while preparing the filling.

Filling:

¾ pound cream cheese	⅓ cup beer
½ cup sugar	⅛ teaspoon salt
2 egg yolks	2 egg whites, stiffly beaten
1 tablespoon flour	

Preheat oven to 350°.

Beat the cream cheese until fluffy. Add the sugar and beat. Beat in the egg yolks, flour, and then the beer and salt. The mixture should be light and well blended. Fold in the egg whites. Turn into the prepared pie plate and bake 30 minutes or until delicately browned and set. (The top may crack slightly.) Turn off the heat and let cake cool in the oven for 10 minutes before removing.

The filling may also be baked in a pastry shell if preferred.

BROWNIES

1 cup sifted cake flour	2 eggs
½ cup unsweetened cocoa	⅛ teaspoon salt
¼ pound butter	½ cup beer
1¼ cups brown sugar, packed	1 cup pecans

Preheat oven to 350°.

Sift together the flour and cocoa. Cream the butter; gradually add the brown sugar, beating until light and fluffy. Add the eggs and salt; beat until well blended. Add the flour mixture alternately with the beer. Stir in the pecans.

Bake in a greased 8-inch-square pan 30 minutes, or until a cake tester comes out clean. Cut into squares while warm.

GINGERBREAD

1¼ cups sifted flour	1 egg
1 teaspoon baking soda	⅓ cup dark brown sugar
¼ teaspoon baking powder	⅓ cup molasses
½ teaspoon salt	⅓ cup melted butter
1½ teaspoons ginger	½ cup beer
½ teaspoon cinnamon	

Preheat oven to 350°.

Sift together the flour, soda, baking powder, salt, ginger, and cinnamon.

Beat the egg; gradually add the brown sugar, molasses, and

butter. Beat until light. Add the dry ingredients alternately with the beer. Turn into a greased 8-inch-square pan.

Bake 30 minutes, or until a cake tester comes out clean. Cut into squares.

DELICATE FRUIT CAKE

1½ cups sifted flour	¼ cup seedless raisins
¾ teaspoon baking powder	¾ cup coarsely chopped
¼ teaspoon baking soda	walnuts
⅛ teaspoon salt	¼ pound butter
1 teaspoon cinnamon	¾ cup brown sugar, packed
½ teaspoon ground ginger	1 egg
½ teaspoon nutmeg	1 cup beer
¾ cup chopped candied fruit	

Preheat oven to 350°.

Sift together the flour, baking powder, soda, salt, cinnamon, ginger, and nutmeg. Mix the fruits, raisins, and nuts with a little of the flour mixture.

Cream the butter, gradually adding the brown sugar, then the egg. Beat until light and fluffy. Add a little of the flour mixture alternately with the beer, mixing lightly. Blend in the fruit-nut mixture. Turn into a buttered 10-inch loaf pan.

Bake 1 hour, or until a cake tester comes out clean. Cool in the pan for 20 minutes, then carefully turn out onto a cake rack. Let stand 24 hours before serving.

GINGER COOKIES

2 cups sifted flour	¾ cup sugar
⅛ teaspoon salt	¾ cup (6 ounces) butter
2 teaspoons baking powder	2 tablespoons molasses
1 tablespoon ground ginger	¼ cup beer

Preheat oven to 400°.

Sift together the flour, salt, baking powder, ginger, and sugar. Work in the butter by hand. Mix the molasses and beer together and add, mixing until a dough is formed.

Roll out as thin as possible on a lightly floured surface. Cut into desired shape and arrange on a buttered cooky sheet, leaving about 1 inch between each. Place a nut in the center of each if desired.

Bake 10 minutes, or until crisp and browned.

Makes about 48 2½-inch cookies.

PLUM PUDDING

½ cup sifted flour
1 teaspoon salt
½ teaspoon baking soda
1 teaspoon cinnamon
½ teaspoon nutmeg
¼ teaspoon ground cloves
2 cups chopped candied
    fruit and peels
1 cup seedless raisins

⅔ cup ale or beer
4 eggs
1⅓ cups dark brown sugar,
    packed
¾ cup coarsely ground nuts
    (Brazil or almonds)
⅓ cup dry bread crumbs
¼ pound (1 cup) ground
    suet (beef fat)

Sift together the flour, salt, baking soda, cinnamon, nutmeg, and cloves.

Combine the candied fruit, raisins, and ale in a bowl; let soak 1 hour.

Beat the eggs, gradually adding the brown sugar. Beat until light and fluffy. Stir in the fruit-ale mixture, nuts, bread crumbs, and suet. Mix. Add the dry ingredients, mixing until well blended.

This amount makes 2 quarts, so use the size mold or molds you prefer. Cover tightly and steam in constantly boiling water 2½ hours for pint molds, 3 hours for a quart mold, and 4 hours for 2-quart mold. Remove from steamer and uncover at once. Let cool

30 minutes before removing from mold. If prepared in advance, cool completely before returning to clean molds. Wrap and store until needed. Steam ½ hour when ready to serve.

Serve warm with vanilla or hard sauce.

Serves 12.

HONEY CAKE

2 eggs	⅛ teaspoon salt
¼ cup sugar	¾ teaspoon baking powder
1 cup honey	½ teaspoon baking soda
¼ cup beer	¼ teaspoon ground ginger
2 tablespoons salad oil	⅛ teaspoon mace
1¾ cups sifted flour	1 cup almonds, split lengthwise

Preheat oven to 325°. Grease a 9-inch loaf pan and dust it lightly with flour.

Beat the eggs until thick. Add the sugar and beat until light and fluffy. Beat in the honey, beer, and oil.

Sift together the flour, salt, baking powder, soda, ginger, and mace. Add to the honey mixture a little at a time, beating lightly after each addition. When about ¼ cup is left, mix the almonds with it and then stir into the batter. Turn into the pan.

Bake 55 minutes, or until a cake tester comes out clean. Cool for 5 minutes in the pan, then turn out and cool on a cake rack.

RAISIN CAKE

1 cup seedless raisins	1 teaspoon cinnamon
1 cup beer	¼ teaspoon nutmeg
3 cups sifted cake flour	½ cup shortening
½ teaspoon salt	1¼ cups sugar
1 tablespoon baking powder	2 egg yolks
¼ teaspoon baking soda	2 egg whites, stiffly beaten

Soak the raisins in the beer for 20 minutes. Sift together the flour, salt, baking powder, baking soda, cinnamon, and nutmeg.

Cream the shortening; gradually add the sugar, beating until fluffy. Beat in 1 egg yolk at a time. Add the dry ingredients alternately with the beer-raisin mixture. Fold in the egg whites.

Turn into 2 greased 9-inch layer cake pans and bake in a 375° oven 30 minutes, or until a cake tester comes out clean.

RAISIN PIE

Pastry for 2-crust pie	½ teaspoon salt
1 pound seedless raisins	½ cup orange juice
1½ cups beer	1 tablespoon lemon juice
½ cup sugar	2 teaspoons grated lemon rind
2 tablespoons quick-cooking tapioca	½ cup coarsely chopped walnuts

Line an 8-inch pie plate with half the pastry.

Combine raisins, beer, sugar, tapioca, and salt in a saucepan. Bring to a boil and cook over low heat, stirring occasionally until tapioca is translucent. Cool. Stir in the orange juice, lemon juice, rind, and walnuts.

Turn into a prepared pie plate and cover with remaining pastry. Bake in a 400° oven 45 minutes, or until delicately browned.

PEAKED ICING

½ cup beer	⅛ teaspoon cream of tartar
1½ cups brown sugar	2 egg whites
⅛ teaspoon salt	

Cook the beer, sugar, salt, and cream of tartar until a little of the mixture dropped into cold water forms a soft ball (238° F.).

Beat the egg whites until stiff. Gradually add the beer mixture, beating constantly until icing forms peaks.

Will ice a 9-inch layer cake.

SPICE CAKE

2¼ cups sifted flour	¼ teaspoon ground allspice
1 tablespoon baking powder	¼ pound butter
¼ teaspoon salt	1 cup sugar
1 teaspoon cinnamon	2 eggs
½ teaspoon ground ginger	⅓ cup molasses
⅛ teaspoon ground cloves	¾ cup beer

Preheat oven to 375°. Butter 2 9-inch layer-cake pans and dust lightly with flour.

Sift together the flour, baking powder, salt, cinnamon, ginger, cloves, and allspice.

Cream the butter, gradually adding the sugar. Beat until light and fluffy. Add 1 egg at a time, beating well after each addition. Stir in the molasses. Add the flour mixture alternately with the beer, stirring until smooth. Divide between the pans.

Bake 30 minutes, or until a cake tester comes out clean. Cool on a cake rack and frost with butter cream.

SWEET POTATO PUDDING

3 cups mashed sweet potatoes	½ teaspoon ground ginger
¾ cup brown sugar	3 eggs, beaten
¼ cup molasses	2 tablespoons melted butter
½ teaspoon salt	¾ cup beer
¼ teaspoon nutmeg	¾ cup heavy cream
1 teaspoon cinnamon	2 teaspoons grated orange rind

Beat all the ingredients together until smooth and fluffy. Turn into a buttered 1½-quart baking dish.

Bake in a 350° oven 1 hour. Serve warm.

Serves 6.

SWEDISH BEER DESSERT

¼ cup flour
2 cups milk
2 cups light cream
1 cup beer

¼ cup molasses
¼ teaspoon ground ginger
4 cardamon seeds

Mix the flour with a little milk to a smooth paste. Add the remaining milk and the cream. Cook over low heat, stirring constantly, to the boiling point. Cook 10 minutes.

In another saucepan, bring to a boil the beer, molasses, ginger, and cardamon seeds. Beat into the milk mixture with a rotary beater until frothy. Serve in mugs or soup plates.

Serves 5–6.

Note: Although a soup for dessert is unusual to Americans, it is a classic Swedish dish.

Foods with Beer

FOODS WITH BEER

For more than six thousand years beer has been the world's favorite beverage—the drink served at great banquets down through the ages.

Brillat-Savarin, one of the most celebrated gourmets of all times, once wrote that the invention of a new dish did more for the happiness of mankind than the discovery of a new star. The proper drink is just as important as a new dish.

There are certain nationalistic styles of cooking that are particularly enhanced by beer—those of Germany, Mexico, and India come readily to mind. In fact, all spicy, highly seasoned dishes are ideal with cooling, thirst-quenching beer. Seafood, whether at home or at a clambake, has a definite affinity with beer. Experts agree that beer refreshes the palate, renewing the inherent flavor of the food.

The recipes in the following section are gathered from many countries. They represent a selection of the wide variety of dishes that may be served with beer for pleasurable dining. Chill the beer in attractive coolers and serve it in the finest crystal at the most formal dinner parties. Beer is equally ideal for the spur-of-the-moment gathering or at a lavish, seated dinner party.

APPETIZERS

ANCHOVY AND CHEESE STRAWS

18 slices white bread
¼ pound cream cheese
3 tablespoons heavy cream
¼ teaspoon freshly ground
　black pepper

18 anchovy fillets
¼ cup melted butter

Buy thinly sliced bread and trim the slices. Wet a towel with cold water and flatten the slices on it with a rolling pin.

Beat together the cream cheese, cream, and pepper; spread on the bread slices. Place an anchovy fillet lengthwise in the center and roll up like a jelly roll. Arrange on a baking sheet. Brush with the melted butter.

Just before serving, toast in a 450° oven until browned.

CHEESE BOWS

2 cups sifted flour
1 tablespoon baking powder
1 teaspoon salt
½ cup shortening

½ cup grated American cheese
⅔ cup milk
Caraway seeds

Preheat oven to 425°.

Sift the flour, baking powder, and salt into a bowl. Cut in the shortening with a pastry blender or 2 knives, then cut in the cheese. Add the milk, tossing until a ball of dough is formed. Knead lightly on a lightly-floured surface, then roll out ⅛ inch thick. Cut into strips ½ inch wide by 6 inches long. Tie loosely and place on a baking sheet 1 inch apart. Sprinkle with caraway seeds.

Bake 10 minutes, or until browned.

Makes about 36.

SWISS CHEESE CRUSTS

¾ pound Swiss cheese, grated
2 egg yolks
½ teaspoon salt
¼ teaspoon freshly ground
   black pepper
2 egg whites, stiffly beaten
12 thin slices white bread,
   trimmed
Fat for deep frying

Blend the cheese, egg yolks, salt, and pepper until smooth. Fold in the egg whites thoroughly. Spread the mixture on 6 slices of the bread. Cover with the remaining slices, pressing down firmly. If desired, secure sandwiches with toothpicks.

Gently place sandwiches in fat heated to 375°. Fry until lightly browned on both sides. Drain. Remove toothpicks if used.

Serves 6.

*   *   *

A keg of beer was the only proper gift to be offered to the Pharaoh by a suitor seeking the hand of a royal princess.

CHEESE STICKS

¼ pound butter
3 tablespoons blue cheese
6 slices Swiss cheese

Cream together the butter and blue cheese. Spread evenly on the Swiss cheese. Chill until creamed mixture is very firm. With a sharp knife, cut into narrow strips.

Makes about 60 Cheese Sticks.

GINGER ALMONDS

2 cups blanched almonds   ¾ teaspoon ground ginger
¼ pound butter   1 teaspoon salt

Be sure the almonds are dry. Melt the butter in a skillet; add the almonds and cook over low heat, stirring almost constantly with a wooden spoon until delicately browned. Remove from the heat and sprinkle with the ginger and salt. Let cool, stirring occasionally.

INDIAN POTATO STRAWS

3 large potatoes   ½ teaspoon turmeric
Fat for deep frying   1 teaspoon chili powder
1½ teaspoons salt
1 teaspoon ground caraway
   seeds

Pare and wash the potatoes; cut them in half lengthwise and grate on a long grater (the straws should be almost shoestring in shape). Wash the grated potatoes under running water and dry on a towel. Heat the fat to 370° and fry a handful of potatoes at a time. Drain and sprinkle with the salt, caraway seeds, turmeric, and chili powder.

ANCHOIADE

4 cans anchovy fillets
3 tablespoons minced parsley
2 cloves garlic, minced
2 tablespoons olive oil

1 tablespoon lemon juice
6 slices white toast, trimmed
and cut in triangles

Finely mash the undrained anchovies. Blend in the parsley, garlic, olive oil, and lemon juice. Heap on the toast and arrange on a greased baking sheet. Bake in a 500° oven for 3 minutes. Serve hot. Makes 18.

SHRIMP TOAST

1 pound cooked shrimp
¼ cup minced scallions or
onions
4 tablespoons mayonnaise
2 hard-cooked eggs, chopped

¼ teaspoon freshly ground
black pepper
6 slices buttered toast, quartered
½ cup grated Parmesan cheese

Chop or grind the shrimp and blend in the scallions, mayonnaise, eggs, and pepper. Taste for seasoning and heap on the toast squares. Sprinkle with the cheese.

Broil in a 350° oven for about 5 minutes, or until delicately browned.

CODFISH FRITTERS

½ pound dried codfish
Fritter Batter (see recipe)
1 clove garlic, minced

¼ teaspoon freshly ground
black pepper
Fat for deep frying

Wash the codfish and soak in water to cover 12–24 hours or overnight. Change the water a few times. Drain and add fresh water to cover; bring to a boil and cook over medium heat 1 hour. Drain. Cool and shred. Add to the Fritter Batter with the garlic and pepper.

Heat the fat to 385° and drop the batter into it by the tablespoon. Fry until browned; drain and serve hot.

Makes about 36.

CROÛTE A LA PROVENÇALE

½ cup minced onion
3 tablespoons olive oil
4 tomatoes, peeled and chopped
1 teaspoon salt
½ teaspoon freshly ground
    black pepper
¼ teaspoon basil
1 clove garlic, minced

1 tablespoon minced parsley
6 slices bread, trimmed
4 tablespoons butter
18 black olives, sliced
12 anchovies
4 tablespoons dry bread
    crumbs

Sauté the onion in olive oil for 5 minutes. Add the tomatoes, salt, pepper, basil and garlic. Cook over low heat 15 minutes, stirring frequently. Stir in the parsley.

Cut each slice of bread into 4 triangles and sauté in the butter until browned on both sides. Spread with the tomato mixture and arrange the sliced olives and anchovies on top. Sprinkle with bread crumbs. Arrange on a baking sheet and bake in a 425° oven 5 minutes.

A delicious change from pizza.

Makes 24.

PROVENÇAL ONION TARTS (*Pissaladière*)

1 package hot-roll mix
½ cup olive oil

6 cups diced onions
1½ teaspoons salt

¾ teaspoon freshly ground
  black pepper
1 cup sliced black olives
  (salty Greek type)

2 cans anchovies, drained
  and minced

Prepare the hot-roll mix according to the instructions on the package; let rise while preparing the onions.

Heat the oil in a skillet; sauté the onions over low heat until soft and yellow. Stir frequently to keep from browning. Season with salt and pepper.

Roll out the dough ¼-inch thick on a lightly floured surface and fit into an 11 × 16-inch jelly-roll pan. (Make rolls of extra dough, if any.) Let rise again according to instructions. Spread the sautéed onions over the dough and dot with the olives and anchovies.

Bake in a 375° oven for 20 minutes, or until dough is browned. Cut into 2-inch squares. Serve hot.

Makes about 40 squares.

SARDINE TART (*Tarte Provençale*)

3 cups sifted flour
2½ teaspoons salt
1 tablespoon baking powder
¾ cup shortening
2 eggs
⅓ cup milk
1 cup minced onions
1 cup diced green pepper
1 clove garlic, minced
3 tablespoons olive oil

1½ teaspoons freshly ground
  black pepper
1½ teaspoons orégano
2 8-ounce cans tomato sauce
2 cans skinless and boneless
  sardines, drained
6 slices salami, cut julienne
¼ pound Mozzarella cheese,
  sliced thin
½ cup grated Parmesan cheese

Sift the flour, ½ teaspoon salt, and the baking powder into a bowl; work in the shortening with the fingers. Beat the eggs and milk together and add, kneading lightly until a ball of dough is formed. Roll out to fit an 11 × 16-inch baking pan, allowing ½ inch extra to form rim. Chill while preparing the filling.

Sauté the onions, green pepper, and garlic in olive oil for 10 minutes. Add the pepper, orégano, tomato sauce, and remaining salt. Cook over low heat 30 minutes. Cool. Preheat oven to 400°.

Spread the cooled sauce on the dough and arrange the sardines and salami over it. Cover with Mozzarella cheese and sprinkle with the Parmesan cheese.

Bake 25 minutes. Cut into squares or strips and serve hot.

CHEESE MEAT BALLS

1 cup grated Cheddar cheese	½ teaspoon dry mustard
1 pound ground beef	1 tablespoon chopped parsley
¼ teaspoon minced garlic	1 teaspoon Worcestershire
1¼ teaspoons salt	sauce
½ teaspoon freshly ground black pepper	6 tablespoons butter

Blend all the ingredients together and shape into walnut-size balls. Brown the balls in the butter and spear with cocktail picks. Makes about 36.

HAM BEIGNETS

¼ cup butter	¼ cup minced onions
½ cup water	1 tablespoon olive oil
½ teaspoon salt	¼ cup chopped ham
2 cups sifted flour	Fat for deep frying
2 eggs	

In a saucepan combine the butter, water, and salt. Bring to a boil and add the flour all at once. Cook over low heat, stirring steadily, until mixture leaves the sides of the pan. Remove from the heat and add 1 egg at a time, beating until smooth and shiny.

Sauté the onion in oil for 5 minutes. Add to the batter with the ham.

Heat the fat to 370°; drop the batter into the fat by the teaspoonful, a few at a time. Fry until browned. Drain and serve hot. Makes about 36.

CORNED BEEF HASH SPREAD

1 can corned beef hash	⅛ teaspoon Tabasco
1 tablespoon prepared mustard	4 tablespoons ketchup
3 tablespoons pickle relish	

Mash the hash and mix with the mustard, relish, Tabasco sauce, and ketchup. Heat in a saucepan. Heap in a bowl and surround with toast or crackers.

HAM TURNOVERS

3 tablespoons butter	½ teaspoon pepper
2 tablespoons flour	½ cup minced onions
¾ cup milk	1½ cups ground cooked ham
1½ teaspoons salt	Pastry for 2-crust pie

Melt 2 tablespoons butter and stir in the flour. Gradually add the milk, stirring constantly to the boiling point. Add the salt and pepper and cook over low heat 5 minutes.

Sauté the onions in the remaining tablespoon of butter 5 minutes. Add onions and ham to the sauce. Taste for seasoning and cool. Preheat oven to 425°.

Roll out the pastry ¼ inch thick and cut into 4-inch squares. Place a heaping tablespoon of the cooled ham filling on each square and fold over to make a triangle, sealing the edges carefully with egg white or water. Brush with egg white.

Bake 20 minutes, or until browned.

Makes about 12 turnovers.

MEAT PÂTÉ

1 pound calf's liver
1 pound sausage meat
½ pound ham
½ pound cooked tongue
1 onion
2½ teaspoons salt
¾ teaspoon freshly ground
   black pepper

½ teaspoon thyme
⅛ teaspoon Tabasco
1 tablespoon minced parsley
6 slices bacon
2 bay leaves

Using the finest blade of a food chopper, grind the liver, sausage, ham, tongue, and onion. Add the salt, pepper, thyme, Tabasco, and parsley. Mix until well blended.

Line a greased 10-inch loaf pan with bacon. Pack the mixture into it. Place the bay leaves on top and cover the pan with aluminum foil. Set in a shallow pan of water and bake in a 350° oven 1½ hours.

Remove the foil and bay leaves. Place a weight on top of the pâté and chill. Carefully turn out and slice thin.

*   *   *

*A quart of ale is a
dish for a king.*
Shakespeare, The Winter's Tale

*   *   *

HOME-STYLE PORK PÂTÉ

2 cups soft bread crumbs
½ cup milk
1 pound lean ground pork
½ cup sliced onions
1 teaspoon salt
½ teaspoon freshly ground
   black pepper
½ teaspoon orégano

2 teaspoons Worcestershire
   sauce
1 tablespoon olive oil
1½ cups grated Parmesan
   cheese
¼ cup cracker meal
5 egg yolks
5 egg whites, stiffly beaten

Soak the bread crumbs in the milk for 5 minutes, then drain. Grind together the pork, onions, and bread, using the finest blade of the food chopper. Beat in the salt, pepper, orégano, Worcestershire sauce, olive oil, cheese, cracker meal, and egg yolks. Fold in the egg whites. Turn into a greased 10-inch loaf pan.

Bake in a 325° oven 1 hour. Let cool in the pan for a few minutes, then carefully turn out. Chill and slice thin.

TARTAR STEAK BALLS

¾ pound freshly ground sirloin steak
1 clove garlic, minced
¼ cup finely chopped onions
1 teaspoon salt
½ teaspoon freshly ground black pepper
2 tablespoons chopped capers (optional)
1 egg white
4 tablespoons minced parsley

Be sure all the fat has been removed from the meat before grinding it. Add the garlic, onions, salt, pepper, and capers. Mix lightly; shape into walnut-size balls. Dip in egg white, then parsley. Spear with a cocktail pick.

Makes about 36.

STUFFED MUSHROOMS

2 pounds mushrooms
¼ cup butter
¼ cup chopped onion
1 clove garlic, minced
1¼ pound ground beef
1 tablespoon anchovy paste
1 tablespoon minced parsley
1 teaspoon salt
½ teaspoon freshly ground black pepper
4 tablespoons olive oil

Select mushrooms that are uniform in size; you should have about 36. Remove the stems and chop coarsely. Melt the butter in a skillet and sauté the onion and chopped stems for 5 minutes. Add the garlic and beef; cook over high heat 2 minutes, stirring constantly. Blend in the anchovy paste, parsley, salt, and pepper. Stuff the mushroom caps.

Heat the oil in a shallow baking pan and arrange mushrooms stuffed side up.

Bake in a 450° oven 15 minutes. Spear with cocktail picks.

FISH AND SHELLFISH

FISH AND CHIPS

4 fillets of sole
¾ cup flour
2 teaspoons salt
½ teaspoon freshly ground
  black pepper

2 eggs, beaten
¾ cup corn meal
Fat for deep frying

Cut the fillets in 2-inch strips. Mix together the flour, salt, and pepper. Dip the strips in the seasoned flour, next in the eggs, and then the corn meal.

Heat the fat to 380° and fry a few pieces at a time until browned. Drain and serve with French-fried potatoes, homemade or frozen.

To retain the "fish and chips" mood, serve in cone-shaped aluminum foil or parchment paper.

Serves 4–8.

DEVILED MACKEREL

6 mackerel fillets
6 tablespoons prepared mustard
1½ teaspoons salt
¼ teaspoon Tabasco sauce

⅛ teaspoon nutmeg
¾ cup dry bread crumbs
2 tablespoons salad oil
4 tablespoons butter

Wash and dry the fillets. Make a paste of the mustard, salt, Tabasco sauce, and nutmeg and rub into the fish. Roll fillets in the bread crumbs.

Heat the oil and butter in a skillet; sauté the fish over low heat until browned on both sides. Serve with lime or lemon wedges. Serves 6.

SALMON IN CURRIED CREAM SAUCE

6 small salmon steaks	2 tablespoons curry powder
½ cup flour	¼ pound butter
1 teaspoon salt	1 cup chopped onions
¼ teaspoon pepper	1 cup sour cream

Wash and dry the salmon; dip in a mixture of the flour, salt, pepper, and 1 tablespoon curry powder.

Melt half the butter in a skillet; sauté the salmon over low heat until browned on both sides and fish flakes easily. Arrange on a platter.

While the fish is cooking, melt the remaining butter in another skillet. Sauté the onions until transparent; sprinkle with the remaining curry powder and stir in the sour cream. Heat, but do not let boil. Pour over the fish.

Serves 6.

SAN PEDRO TUNA PIE

Pastry for 1-crust pie	½ teaspoon freshly ground
¾ cup olive oil	black pepper
2 cups diced onions	4 tablespoons minced parsley
½ pound mushrooms, chopped	2 cans (7¾ ounces) tuna fish,
1 can (8 ounces) tomato sauce	drained and flaked
1 teaspoon salt	4 pimientos, cut julienne

Preheat oven to 375°.

Roll out the pastry and fit into a 9-inch pie plate. Flute the edges and prick the bottom. Set another pie plate over it to keep it from shrinking. Bake 20 minutes. Meanwhile prepare the filling.

Heat the olive oil and sauté the onions 10 minutes. Add the mushrooms and sauté 5 minutes. Stir in the tomato sauce, salt, and pepper. Cook over low heat 5 minutes. Remove from heat and stir in the parsley, tuna, and pimientos. Cool slightly and pour into the shell.

Bake 20 minutes. Serve hot, cut into wedges.

Serves 6–8.

CLAM SAUTÉ

36 clams, shucked	½ teaspoon freshly ground
½ pound butter	black pepper
1 teaspoon salt	½ teaspoon paprika
2 teaspoons Worcestershire sauce	2 tablespoons minced parsley

Drain the clams very well. Melt the butter in a skillet; sauté the clams 5 minutes, stirring frequently. Season with salt, Worcestershire sauce, pepper, and paprika. Serve on buttered toast, sprinkled with parsley.

Serves 2–6.

CLAMS WITH RICE SAUCE

36 clams, in the shell	1½ cups chicken broth
1 cup minced onions	1 tablespoon lemon juice
1 clove garlic, minced	3 tablespoons minced parsley
½ cup raw rice	⅛ teaspoon Tabasco
¼ cup olive oil	

Scrub the clams and rinse in cold water.

Sauté the onions, garlic, and rice in the oil until the rice is transparent, stirring almost constantly. Add the broth, lemon juice, parsley, and Tabasco. Cover and cook over low heat 10 minutes.

Add the clams; cover again and cook 10 minutes longer, or until clams open and rice is tender. Serve in deep dishes.
Serves 4–6.

BAYOU STUFFED CRABS

1 pound crab meat	1 cup heavy cream
½ cup minced onions	1 tablespoon chili sauce
½ pound mushrooms, coarsely	1 tablespoon finely chopped
chopped	chives or scallions
3 tablespoons butter	⅛ teaspoon Tabasco
2 tablespoons flour	1 tablespoon lemon juice
1½ teaspoons salt	2 egg whites, stiffly beaten
¼ teaspoon freshly ground	⅓ cup bread crumbs
black pepper	2 tablespoons melted butter

Use 6 crab shells or ramekins for baking. Pick over the crab meat, removing any tendons. Preheat oven to 400°.

Sauté onions and mushrooms in the butter 5 minutes, stirring occasionally. Sprinkle with the flour, salt, and pepper. Stir constantly until flour turns golden brown. Gradually add the cream, stirring constantly to the boiling point. Blend in the chili sauce, chives, Tabasco sauce, lemon juice, and crab meat. Cook over low heat 5 minutes. Taste for seasoning. Cool 10 minutes.

Fold in the egg whites. Turn into the shells or ramekins. Sprinkle with the bread crumbs and melted butter.

Bake 10 minutes or until delicately browned.

MARYLAND CRAB CAKES

¾ cup olive oil	2 teaspoons Worcestershire
6 slices bread, trimmed	sauce
3 egg yolks	1½ pounds crab meat
¾ teaspoon salt	3 egg whites, stiffly beaten
⅛ teaspoon Tabasco sauce	4 tablespoons butter

Pour the oil over the bread and let soak 15 minutes. Mash the bread and add the egg yolks, salt, Tabasco, and Worcestershire. Blend in the crab meat and fold in the egg whites. Shape into 12 or 18 cakes.

Melt half the butter in a skillet and brown the cakes on both sides, adding butter as needed.

For hot hors d'oeuvre, make smaller cakes.

SOUTHERN FRIED OYSTERS

2 dozen oysters
¾ cup sifted yellow or white corn meal
¼ cup dry bread crumbs
¼ teaspoon pepper
2 eggs, beaten
Fat for deep frying

Drain the oysters and dry between towels. Mix together the corn meal, bread crumbs, and pepper. Dip the oysters first in the eggs and then the corn-meal mixture, coating them thoroughly.

Heat the fat to 375° and fry the oysters until browned, about 2 minutes. Drain. Delicious with corn bread and salad.

Serves 4.

CRUSTED SCALLOPS

1½ pounds scallops
2 tablespoons vinegar
3 cups boiling water
1 cup dry bread crumbs
½ cup cracker meal
1½ teaspoons salt
⅛ teaspoon cayenne pepper
2 eggs, beaten
6 slices bacon, chopped

Buy bay scallops if they are available. If sea scallops are used, they should be quartered. Wash and drain. Let the scallops soak in the vinegar and boiling water 3 minutes. Drain.

Mix together the bread crumbs, cracker meal, salt, and cayenne pepper. Roll the scallops in the mixture, then dip in the eggs and again in the crumbs, coating them well. Arrange in a greased baking dish and sprinkle the bacon over all.

Bake in a 450° oven 10 minutes, or until browned.

Serves 6.

COCONUT SHRIMP

½ cup grated coconut	1½ teaspoons salt
2 pounds shrimp, shelled and deveined	½ teaspoon paprika
	1 bay leaf
4 tablespoons butter	3 tablespoons currants
¼ cup sliced, blanched almonds	¾ cup heavy cream

If dried coconut is used, wash it under running water to remove the sweetness. Wash and dry the shrimp.

Melt half the butter in a skillet; lightly brown the almonds and coconut. Remove. Melt the remaining butter in the same skillet; sauté the shrimp on both sides. Return the coconut and almonds and add the salt, paprika, bay leaf, currants, and cream. Bring to a boil and cook over low heat 5 minutes.

Serves 4–6.

DEVILED SHRIMP

2 pounds raw shrimp, shelled and deveined	½ cup dry bread crumbs
1 teaspoon dry mustard	2 tablespoons grated onion
1 teaspoon salt	2 tablespoons minced parsley
⅓ cup olive or salad oil	⅛ teaspoon Tabasco

Wash and dry the shrimp and arrange them in a shallow baking dish. Mix together the mustard, salt, and oil; brush the shrimp with some of the mixture.

Broil at 400° for 3 minutes and turn the shrimp. Brush with

the remaining oil mixture and coat with a mixture of the bread crumbs, onion, parsley, and Tabasco sauce. Broil 3 minutes more.

Serves 6 as an appetizer, or pierce with cocktail picks and serve as an hors d'oeuvre.

BROILED SPICY SHRIMP

2 pounds raw shrimp, shelled and deveined	2 teaspoons chili powder
1½ teaspoons salt	½ teaspoon orégano
¼ teaspoon freshly ground black pepper	3 cloves garlic, minced
	1 cup olive or salad oil
	1 tablespoon vinegar

Wash and dry the shrimp. In a bowl, mix together all the ingredients and marinate the shrimp overnight, or at least 3 hours.

Arrange the shrimp in a shallow pan and pour the marinade over them. Broil 5–6 minutes, turning them once. Serve hot.

Serves 6–8 as an appetizer.

SHRIMP IN GARLIC SAUCE

½ cup olive oil	4 cloves garlic, minced
2 pounds raw shrimp, shelled and deveined	¼ cup minced parsley
1½ teaspoons salt	1 tablespoon butter
½ teaspoon freshly ground black pepper	1 teaspoon lemon juice

Heat the oil in a skillet; sauté the shrimp on both sides 5 minutes. Sprinkle with the salt and pepper and transfer to a heated platter.

Add the garlic, parsley, butter, and lemon juice to the oil in the skillet and cook until butter melts. Pour over the shrimp and serve. Serves 4–6.

SHRIMP, TAHITIAN STYLE

1 cup shredded coconut	1 cup flour
2 pounds raw shrimp	1 teaspoon baking powder
¼ cup lemon juice	⅔ cup milk
1½ teaspoons curry powder	¼ cup cornstarch
1½ teaspoons salt	Fat for deep frying
½ teaspoon ground ginger	

Spread the coconut on a baking pan and bake in a 300° oven 15 minutes.

Shell the shrimp but do not remove the tail. Slit the back and remove the black vein under running water. Drain well. Mix together the lemon juice, curry powder, 1 teaspoon salt, and the ginger. Pour over the shrimp and let marinate overnight, or at least 4 hours. Drain, reserving the marinade.

Beat together the flour, baking powder, milk, and remaining salt. Stir in the marinade. Toss the shrimp with the cornstarch, then dip them in the batter and roll in the coconut.

Heat the fat to 380° and fry the shrimp until browned. Drain and serve hot with Chinese *duk* sauce, curry sauce, or minced chutney.

Serves 6–8 as a first course. Also delicious as a hot hors d'oeuvre.

OLD-FASHIONED SEAFOOD BAKE

2 tablespoons butter	½ cup minced onions
2 tablespoons flour	2 tablespoons bread crumbs
1 cup milk	1 cup sour cream
1½ teaspoons salt	1½ pounds shrimp, cooked and
¼ teaspoon pepper	cleaned
1 teaspoon paprika	1 cup cooked green peas
1½ pounds crab meat	Pastry for 1 crust

Melt the butter in a saucepan; stir in the flour and then gradually add the milk, mixing steadily to the boiling point. Season with the salt, pepper, and paprika and cook over low heat 5 minutes. Preheat oven to 400°.

Mix together the crab meat, onions, bread crumbs and sour cream. In a buttered, deep 9-inch pie plate or baking dish arrange successive layers of the crab meat, shrimp, and peas. Pour the sauce over all. Roll out the pastry, and cover the pie plate with it.

Bake 30 minutes, or until browned. Serve directly from the pie plate. Cut in wedges.

Serves 6.

SEAFOOD CREOLE

¾ cup minced onion	1 bay leaf
2 tablespoons olive oil	1 tablespoon cornstarch
¾ cup sliced mushrooms	¼ cup minced pimiento
½ cup chopped green pepper	2 tablespoons minced parsley
1 20-ounce can tomatoes	1 pound raw shrimp, shelled
1½ teaspoons salt	and deveined
½ teaspoon freshly ground	½ pound crab meat
black pepper	

Sauté the onion in the oil 10 minutes. Add the mushrooms and green pepper; sauté 3 minutes. Stir in the tomatoes, salt, pepper, and bay leaf. Cover and cook over low heat 1 hour.

Mix the cornstarch with a little water; add to the sauce, stirring constantly to the boiling point. Add the pimiento, parsley, and shrimp; cook 5 minutes. Add the crab meat and heat. Taste for seasoning.

Serves 6.

POULTRY

BAKED PUNGENT BROILERS

2 1½-pound broilers	1 teaspoon ground ginger
½ cup soy sauce	2 tablespoons sesame seeds
½ cup honey	1 cup chicken broth
¼ teaspoon pepper	

Wash, dry, and quarter the broilers. Mix together the soy sauce, honey, pepper, ginger, and sesame seeds. Let broilers stand 1 hour in the mixture, turning them to coat well.

Arrange the chicken in a shallow greased baking dish. Mix the broth with the soy mixture and pour over the chicken.

Bake in a 350° oven 40 minutes, or until tender and browned, basting frequently.

Serves 4.

CHICKEN-LENTIL CASSEROLE

2 cups lentils (red, if available)	1 4-pound roasting chicken, disjointed
2 cloves	4 tablespoons oil
1 onion	3 cups chicken broth
1 bay leaf	¼ teaspoon orégano
¼ cup flour	4 Italian sausages, sliced
3 teaspoons salt	
¾ teaspoon freshly ground black pepper	

Wash the lentils and combine in a saucepan with the cloves stuck in the onion, the bay leaf and water to cover. Bring to a boil and cook over low heat 1 hour, or until lentils are almost tender. Drain.

Mix the flour with 1½ teaspoons salt and ¼ teaspoon pepper. Roll the chicken in the seasoned flour.

Heat the oil in a Dutch oven or casserole and brown the chicken on all sides. Add the lentils, broth, orégano, and remaining salt and pepper. Cover.

Bake in a 350° oven 1 hour. Brown the sausages and arrange on top of the lentils. Cover and bake 30 minutes longer, or until chicken is tender.

Serves 4–6.

HAWAIIAN STUFFED CHICKEN

2 1½-pound whole broilers	3 tablespoons soy sauce
2 teaspoons salt	½ teaspoon powdered ginger
½ teaspoon pepper	¾ cup diced water chestnuts
4 slices white bread, trimmed	2 tablespoons salad oil
1 cup light cream	1 cup pineapple juice
¼ pound ground beef	2 tablespoons honey
½ pound ground veal	½ cup sesame seeds
4 tablespoons minced onion	

Wash, and dry the chickens. Sprinkle with the salt and pepper.

Soak the bread in the cream; press out the liquid and mash the bread. Mix together the beef, veal, onion, soy sauce, ginger, water chestnuts, and bread. Stuff the broilers and close the openings with skewers, thread, or aluminum foil.

Oil a shallow baking pan and roast chickens in a 400° oven 20 minutes. Mix the pineapple juice and honey and pour over the chicken. Reduce the heat to 350° and roast 35 minutes longer, basting frequently. Sprinkle the sesame seeds on the chicken and roast in a 450° oven 5 minutes, or until browned. Cut each chicken in half and serve with sautéed pineapple.

Serves 4.

CHICKEN WITH ORANGES AND PEPPERS

1 3½-pound fryer, disjointed
¼ cup olive oil
3 onions, sliced
2 cloves garlic, minced
2 teaspoons salt
½ teaspoon freshly ground
    black pepper
¼ teaspoon dried marjoram

¼ teaspoon dried thyme
½ cup water
4 green peppers, cut julienne
3 tomatoes, diced
¼ teaspoon dried basil
2 oranges, peeled and sliced
    crosswise

Wash and dry the chicken. Heat the oil in a deep skillet; brown the chicken and onions. Add the garlic, salt, pepper, marjoram, thyme, and water. Cover and cook over low heat 30 minutes. Add the peppers, tomatoes, and basil. Cook 30 minutes longer, or until chicken is tender, adding a little more water if pan becomes dry. Arrange the orange slices on top and heat 5 minutes.
Serves 4.

CHICKEN PILAU

1½ cups raw rice
4 tablespoons butter
2 onions, thinly sliced
2 cloves garlic, minced
2 1½-pound chickens,
    quartered

2 teaspoons salt
½ teaspoon ground ginger
2 teaspoons curry powder
2 cups yogurt
2 cups chicken broth

Wash the rice in several waters and drain well.

Melt the butter in a casserole or Dutch oven. Sauté the onions and garlic 10 minutes, stirring frequently. Add the chickens and brown on all sides. Add the salt, ginger, curry powder, yogurt, and broth. Mix well. Place the rice on top. The liquid should just cover the rice; if not, add a little water. Bring to a boil; cover tightly and cook over low heat 35 minutes, or until chicken and rice are tender.
Serves 6.

FRIED CHICKEN, PARMA STYLE

1 2½-pound fryer, disjointed, or	1 egg
4 chicken breasts	2 tablespoons milk
¼ cup flour	½ cup dried bread crumbs
2 teaspoons salt	½ cup grated Parmesan cheese
¼ teaspoon pepper	¼ pound butter

Wash and dry the chicken; roll in a mixture of flour, salt, and pepper. Beat together the egg and milk; combine the bread crumbs and cheese. Dip the chicken in the egg mixture and then in the cheese mixture.

Melt the butter in a skillet. Sauté the chicken until lightly browned on all sides, then cook over very low heat 30 minutes, or until tender. Turn the pieces frequently.

Serves 4.

INDONESIAN RICE AND CHICKEN (*Nasi Goreng*)

2½ cups raw rice (long grain)	2 cups cooked small shrimp
3¾ cups chicken broth	½ cup crab meat
1 teaspoon salt	½ teaspoon ground cumin seed
1 bay leaf	2 teaspoons ground coriander
⅓ cup peanut or salad oil	¼ teaspoon nutmeg
2 cups minced onion	¼ teaspoon ginger
2 cloves garlic, minced	½ teaspoon dried, ground chili
2 cups cooked chicken, cut in	peppers
strips	⅓ cup peanut butter
½ cup diced ham	

Wash the rice in several changes of water; combine in a saucepan with the broth, salt, and bay leaf. Cover and cook over low heat 20 minutes, or until rice is tender but firm. Drain if any liquid remains, and chill the rice. (In Indonesia, the rice is cooked the day before it is to be used.)

Heat the oil in a deep skillet; sauté the onion and garlic 10 minutes. Add the rice and cook until browned, stirring frequently. Stir in the chicken, ham, shrimp, crab meat, cumin, coriander, nutmeg, ginger, chili peppers, and peanut butter. Cook over low heat 10 minutes, stirring almost constantly.

Serve with Sambals. See recipes.

Serves 6–8.

CHICKEN LIVERS WITH APPLES AND ONIONS

1 pound chicken livers	1 large onion, sliced thin
4 tablespoons flour	2 apples, sliced ½ inch thick
1 teaspoon salt	2 tablespoons brown sugar
6 tablespoons butter	

Wash the livers and carefully remove any discolored spots; drain well. Toss the livers in the flour seasoned with salt.

Heat half the butter in a skillet; sauté the livers until browned and cooked the way you like them.

Sauté the onions in half of the remaining butter. Brown the apples in the remaining butter, sprinkling the slices with the sugar to glaze them.

Mix together the livers and onions and arrange the apple slices on top.

Serves 3–4.

TAHITIAN CHICKEN CURRY

1 3½-pound frying chicken	1½ teaspoons salt
4 tablespoons butter	¼ teaspoon white pepper
¾ cup minced onion	2 tablespoons cognac
2 tablespoons flour	1 cup heavy cream
1 cup chicken broth	1 tablespoon curry powder

Wash and dry the chicken; brown in the butter with the onion. Sprinkle with flour and stir in the broth, salt, and pepper. Cover and cook over low heat 1 hour, or until tender. Warm the cognac; set it aflame and pour over the chicken. Shake the pan until flame dies. Transfer the chicken to a serving dish and keep it warm.

Stir the cream and curry powder into the sauce. Cook over high heat 5 minutes. Pour over the chicken.

Serves 4.

ROAST GOOSE WITH APPLE-CHESTNUT STUFFING

12-pound goose	1½ pounds chestnuts, cooked
1 tablespoon salt	and chopped
½ teaspoon pepper	½ cup seedless raisins
2 teaspoons paprika	1 cup soft bread crumbs
½ teaspoon garlic powder	½ teaspoon powdered ginger
1 cup diced onion	½ teaspoon mace
½ cup rendered goose fat or	½ teaspoon nutmeg
butter	2 tablespoons cognac
4 cups diced apples	

Clean the goose; remove as much fat as possible; wash and dry. Mix together the salt, pepper, paprika, and garlic powder. Rub into the goose, inside and out.

Sauté the onion in the fat or butter for 10 minutes. Add the apples, chestnuts, and raisins. Cook over low heat 15 minutes, stirring frequently. Stir in the bread crumbs, ginger, mace, nutmeg, and cognac. Stuff the goose with the mixture, closing the opening with skewers, thread, or aluminum foil.

Place on a rack in a shallow roasting pan and roast in a 425° oven 30 minutes. Pour off the fat. Prick the skin with a fork, reduce the heat to 350°, and roast 3 hours longer, or until goose is tender and browned. Keep pouring off the fat, and after 1½ hours of roasting time, pour 1 cup of ice water over the goose. Baste frequently thereafter.

Serves 8–10.

*　　*　　*

Vassar, the first privately endowed college for women, was founded in 1865 by Matthew Vassar, a brewer of Poughkeepsie, New York. Undergraduates still sing:

> *"And so you see, for old V.C.*
> *Our love shall never fail*
> *Full well we know*
> *That all we owe*
> *To Matthew Vassar's ale!"* *

* Courtesy of Vassar College.

MEAT

DEVILED ROAST BEEF

½ cup flour
1 teaspoon salt
¼ teaspoon pepper
½ teaspoon dry mustard
1 teaspoon chili powder

6 slices cooked roast beef or
roast beef bones
1 egg, beaten
4 tablespoons butter

Mix together the flour, salt, pepper, dry mustard, and chili powder. Dip the roast beef or bones in the egg and then in the flour mixture. Brown quickly in hot butter.

This is an excellent way to change the character of leftover roast beef.

Serves 6.

STEAK IN CRUST

6 slices club steak, ½ inch thick
2 teaspoons salt
½ teaspoon freshly ground
black pepper
2 cloves garlic, minced

2 tablespoons wine vinegar
2 eggs, beaten
1½ cups cracker meal
⅓ cup salad oil

Flatten steak slightly by pounding with a mallet or knife (or have the butcher do it). Mix together 1½ teaspoons salt, the pepper, garlic, and vinegar. Rub into the steak and let stand 1–2 hours before using.

Dip the steaks in the eggs and then the cracker meal mixed with remaining salt. Heat the oil in a skillet and brown the steaks on both sides.

Serves 6.

LONDON BROIL WITH ROQUEFORT CHEESE

1 2-pound flank steak	⅛ teaspoon thyme
1 cup salad oil	1 clove garlic, minced
2 tablespoons wine vinegar	¼ pound Roquefort cheese
1 teaspoon soy sauce	2 tablespoons heavy cream

Buy a very tender flank steak and have it scored. In a bowl, combine the oil, vinegar, soy sauce, thyme, and garlic. Marinate the steak 12–24 hours or overnight, basting and turning it a few times.

Remove from the marinade and place on a greased rack. Broil 2 inches from the heat 5 minutes. Turn and broil other side 4 minutes, then spread with the Roquefort mashed with the cream. Broil 2 minutes longer. Cut diagonally across the grain into very thin slices.

Serves 4–6.

SPICY BEEF STEW

2 tablespoons flour	3 cups sliced onions
1½ teaspoons salt	1 clove garlic, minced
¼ teaspoon pepper	2 teaspoons curry powder
2 pounds top round or chuck cut in 1-inch cubes	1½ cups beef broth
3 tablespoons salad oil	½ cup tomato juice

Combine the flour, salt, and pepper; toss meat in the mixture. Heat the oil in a Dutch oven or heavy saucepan; brown the meat on all sides. Add the onions and garlic and let brown. Stir in the

curry powder and broth. Cover and cook over low heat 1 hour, or until meat is tender. Add the tomato juice and cook 10 minutes longer. Taste for seasoning.
Serves 6–8.

BEEFSTEAK, MONTPARNASSE

4 tablespoons butter	½ pound mushrooms, sliced
4 club or round steaks cut ½ inch thick (about 1¾ pounds)	½ cup dry white wine
	¼ cup beef broth
	1 bay leaf
2 slices bacon, minced	3 tablespoons minced parsley
12 small white onions, half cooked and drained	2 teaspoons salt
	½ teaspoon freshly ground black pepper
1½ cups cubed potatoes	

Melt the butter in a skillet and quickly brown the steak on both sides. Transfer to a casserole with the butter. Add the bacon, onions, potatoes, mushrooms, wine, broth, bay leaf, parsley, salt, and pepper. Cover.

Bake in a 375° oven 45 minutes, or until potatoes are tender. Taste for seasoning; discard bay leaf. Serve with creamed spinach.
Serves 4.

CORNED BEEF HASH

3 potatoes	1 teaspoon salt
4 tablespoons butter	½ teaspoon freshly ground black pepper
1 cup diced onions	
3 cups coarsely chopped cooked corned beef	

Half-cook the potatoes in their jackets; remove the skins and dice very small.

Melt the butter in a large skillet; sauté the onions 5 minutes.

Add the potatoes and cook over low heat 5 minutes. Stir in the corned beef, salt, and pepper. Cook over low heat 20 minutes, stirring occasionally.

For a pancake-style hash, mix the sautéed onions and potatoes with the corned beef. Melt some butter in a skillet and turn the mixture into it. Cook without stirring until underside browns. Turn carefully and brown on other side, or place under a broiler until brown.

Serves 6.

*   *   *

John Alden, the famous John who spoke for himself to Priscilla in colonial America, came to America because he was a cooper by trade, assigned to taking care of beer barrels aboard the Mayflower.

DANISH MEAT BALLS (*Frikadeller*)

1 pound veal	½ teaspoon freshly ground
1½ pounds pork	black pepper
¾ cup sifted flour	1½ cups light cream
1½ teaspoons salt	4 tablespoons butter

Grind the veal and pork 4 times (or have the butcher do it). Add the flour, salt, pepper, and cream; beat together until very light and spongy. Shape tablespoonfuls of the mixture into balls.

Melt the butter in a skillet and sauté the balls over low heat until browned on all sides. Be sure you sauté them over low heat to allow enough time for the meat to cook through.

Serve with mashed potatoes and creamed spinach flavored with mace.

Serves 6.

GOULASH WITH SAUERKRAUT (*Székely Gulyas*)

¼ cup flour	3 tablespoons fat or oil
2 teaspoons salt	3 onions, sliced
½ teaspoon pepper	1 tablespoon paprika
2 pounds veal cut in 2-inch cubes	2 pounds sauerkraut
	1 tablespoon caraway seeds
2 pounds pork cut in 2-inch cubes	½ pint sour cream

Mix together the flour, salt, and pepper; toss the veal and pork in the mixture.

Heat the fat in a heavy saucepan or Dutch oven; brown the meat and onions, then sprinkle with the paprika. Cover and cook over low heat 30 minutes. Watch carefully to prevent burning.

Wash the sauerkraut under running water and drain. Add to the meat along with the caraway seeds and a little water if pan is dry. Cover again and cook over low heat 1½ hours, adding a little water if necessary. Stir in the sour cream and taste for seasoning. Heat but do not let boil.

Serves 6–8.

CHILI CON CARNE

2 cups dried red beans	2 pounds beef in ¼-inch cubes
3 tablespoons olive oil	3 tablespoons chili powder
1 cup chopped onions	1 29-ounce can tomatoes
3 cloves garlic, minced	2 teaspoons salt

Wash the beans and soak in water to cover overnight. Drain and add fresh water to cover. Bring to a boil and cook 2 hours, or until almost tender. Drain. (Four cups canned kidney beans may be substituted.)

Heat the oil in a saucepan; brown the onions, garlic, and beef. Add the chili powder, tomatoes, and salt. Cover and cook over low heat 1½ hours. Add the beans and cook 45 minutes longer. Taste for seasoning. Serve with mounds of rice, shredded lettuce, minced onions, and tortillas or crackers.

Serves 6–8.

IOWA BEEF PIE

¼ cup flour	½ pound mushrooms, sliced
2 teaspoons salt	1½ cups tomato juice
¼ teaspoon pepper	2 bay leaves
¼ teaspoon thyme	2 cups diced potatoes
1½ pounds beef cut in 1-inch cubes	1½ cups shelled green peas, fresh or frozen
3 tablespoons butter	Pastry for 1 crust
½ cup minced onions	

Combine the flour, salt, pepper, and thyme. Toss the meat in the mixture, reserving any extra flour mixture. Brown the meat in the butter; stir in the onions and mushrooms and let brown 5 minutes. Sprinkle with any remaining flour and stir in the tomato juice. Cook over low heat, stirring constantly, to the boiling point. Add the bay leaves; cover and cook over low heat 25 minutes. Add the potatoes and peas; cook 15 minutes longer, adding a little water if necessary, but not too much, as gravy should be thick. Taste for seasoning and discard the bay leaves. Turn into a 1½-quart casserole and cover with the pastry. Slit the top in a few places.

Bake in a 425° oven 20 minutes, or until browned.

Serves 6–8.

PEPPER STEAK

3 pounds round or chuck steak	1 20-ounce can tomatoes
3 tablespoons salad oil	1 can (8 ounces) tomato sauce
2 teaspoons salt	2 bay leaves
¼ teaspoon freshly ground black pepper	¼ teaspoon thyme
	½ cup beef broth
6 green peppers, thinly sliced	2 tablespoons minced parsley
6 onions, thinly sliced	

Have the steak cut about 1 inch thick and then in 2 pieces. Heat the oil in a skillet and brown the steak on both sides.

In a casserole or Dutch oven, place 1 piece of steak, sprinkle with salt and pepper, then add a layer of green pepper and onions. Repeat with the remaining steak, peppers, and onions. Add the tomatoes, tomato sauce, bay leaves, thyme, and broth. Cover and cook over low heat 2 hours, or until tender. Stir once or twice and taste for seasoning. Discard bay leaf.

Serves 6–8.

BARBECUED SHORT RIBS

4 pounds short ribs of beef	1 cup ketchup
⅓ cup flour	½ cup cider vinegar
2 teaspoons salt	2 teaspoons paprika
½ teaspoon freshly ground black pepper	2 teaspoons chili powder
	⅛ teaspoon Tabasco
2 tablespoons salad oil	1 tablespoon sugar
3 onions, sliced	½ teaspoon dry mustard
2 cloves garlic, minced	1 cup beef broth

Cut the ribs in serving-size pieces; roll in a mixture of flour, salt, and pepper.

Heat the oil in a Dutch oven or heavy saucepan; brown the ribs. Add the onions and garlic; brown slightly. Mix together the ketchup, vinegar, paprika, chili powder, Tabasco sauce, sugar, mustard, and beef broth. Add to the ribs; cover. Bake in a 350° oven 2 hours, or until tender. Stir once or twice. Skim the fat.

Serves 6–8.

CHEESE-CHILI BURGERS

1 pound ground beef
1 teaspoon salt
⅛ teaspoon freshly ground black pepper
3 teaspoons chili powder
4 slices American cheese

2 tablespoons olive oil
½ cup minced onions
¼ cup chopped green pepper
1 cup chili sauce
¾ cup water

Mix together the beef, salt, pepper, and 1 teaspoon chili powder. Shape into 8 patties. Place a slice of cheese (cut to fit) on each of 4 patties. Cover with the other patties and press edges together to seal.

Heat the oil in a skillet; brown the patties on both sides. Remove the patties. Sauté the onions and green pepper for 5 minutes; stir in the chili sauce, water, and remaining chili powder. Add the patties. Cover and cook over low heat 10 minutes.

Serves 4.

MEAT RING SOUFFLÉ

¼ pound butter
3 egg yolks
¼ cup cold water
¼ cup wheat germ
1½ pounds ground beef
1 cup finely chopped mushrooms

1½ teaspoons salt
¼ teaspoon pepper
⅛ teaspoon nutmeg
3 egg whites, stiffly beaten

Preheat oven to 350°.

Cream the butter, then add 1 egg yolk at a time, beating until blended. Beat in the water, wheat germ, beef, mushrooms, salt, pepper, and nutmeg. Fold in the egg whites. Turn into a greased 9-inch tube pan. Cover with aluminum foil. Place in a shallow pan of hot • water.

Bake 1 hour, or until set. Carefully run a spatula around the edge of pan. Invert on a heated serving dish, but let it rest a minute or two to allow it to shrink from the sides of the pan, then remove the pan. Serve with mushroom sauce.

Serves 6.

STEAK AND KIDNEY PIE

2 pounds round steak, 1-inch thick	2 onions, diced
½ cup flour	2 carrots, grated
2 teaspoons salt	¼ teaspoon thyme
½ teaspoon pepper	2 cups beef broth
4 tablespoons butter	6 lamb kidneys
	Pastry for 1 crust

Cut the steak in strips 2 inches by 1 inch. Roll in a mixture of the flour, salt, and pepper. Reserve whatever is left of the flour mixture. Melt half the butter in a saucepan and brown the meat. Add the onions and carrots and let brown. Stir in the thyme and broth. Cover and cook over low heat 1 hour, or until meat is tender. Preheat oven to 400°.

Skin the kidneys; split in half and discard the core. Slice thin and roll in the remaining flour mixture. Brown quickly in the remaining butter. Arrange layers of the beef and kidneys in a 2-quart casserole. Add the gravy and enough beef broth to come halfway up. Taste for seasoning.

Roll out the pastry and cover the casserole. Make a few slits on top and seal the edges. Brush with egg yolk or cream.

Bake 30 minutes, or until browned.   Serves 6.

CORNED BEEF AND CABBAGE

4 pounds corned beef	8 peppercorns
2 onions	6 potatoes
2 bay leaves	2 heads cabbage, quartered
2 cloves garlic	

Wash the corned beef under running water. Place in a deep kettle and cover with water. Bring to a boil; skim the top. Add the onions, bay leaves, garlic, and peppercorns. Cover loosely and cook over medium heat 3 hours, or until meat is tender. Place the meat on a platter and keep hot.

Cook the potatoes and cabbage in the stock until tender. Start the potatoes before the cabbage, as you don't want the cabbage to be overcooked. Drain thoroughly and arrange around the meat. Serves 8.

FRICASSEE OF LAMB

3 pounds boneless lamb cut in 2-inch cubes	2 cups sliced onions
1 tablespoon salt	1 20-ounce can tomatoes
½ teaspoon freshly ground black pepper	2 bay leaves
	2 tablespoons capers
½ teaspoon orégano	4 potatoes, peeled and quartered
2 cloves garlic, minced	1½ cups cooked or canned green peas
2 tablespoons lemon juice	½ cup sliced stuffed olives
3 slices bacon, minced	

Remove all the fat from the lamb. Mix together the salt, pepper, orégano, garlic, and lemon juice. Toss the lamb in the mixture and set aside 1–2 hours.

Cook the bacon in a Dutch oven or heavy saucepan until there are about 2 tablespoons of fat in the pan. Add the lamb and onions and cook over high heat until browned, stirring frequently. Stir in the tomatoes, bay leaves, and capers. Cover and cook over low heat 1 hour. Add the potatoes; cook 20 minutes. Add the peas and olives; cook 10 minutes longer, or until lamb is tender.

Serves 6–8.

LAMB AND RICE CASSEROLE

6 loin or shoulder lamb chops
2 cups sliced onions
2 tablespoons salad oil
4 potatoes, pared and sliced
6 tomatoes, sliced
2 green peppers cut in eighths
¾ cup raw rice

3 cups tomato juice
2 teaspoons salt
½ teaspoon freshly ground black pepper
½ teaspoon basil
2 tablespoons minced parsley

Brown the chops in a skillet and drain. While the chops are browning, sauté the onions in the oil until browned. In a casserole, arrange successive layers of onions, potatoes, tomatoes, and green peppers. Pour the rice over the vegetables and then add the tomato juice. Arrange the chops on top. Sprinkle with the salt, pepper, and basil. Cover.

Bake in a 350° oven 45 minutes, basting frequently. Uncover the casserole and bake 15 minutes longer, or until everything is tender. Sprinkle with parsley. Serve with lima beans or lentils.

Serves 6.

Note: Pork chops may be prepared in the same manner.

ROAST LEG OF LAMB

5-pound leg of lamb
1 tablespoon salt
½ teaspoon freshly ground black pepper

1 teaspoon marjoram
2 cloves garlic, minced
2 tablespoons olive oil

Have the fell (skin) removed. Wash and dry the meat and cut a few gashes in the leg. Mix to a paste the salt, pepper, marjoram, garlic, and olive oil. Rub into the meat. (If possible, season the day before for better penetration.)

Roast in a 325° oven 3 hours (30 minutes per pound), or until tender. Baste frequently and add a little water if necessary. Serve with pan gravy.   Serves 6–8.

BRAISED VEAL AND ENDIVE

½ cup flour	4 tablespoons butter
2 teaspoons salt	12 endive
½ teaspoon freshly ground black pepper	1 cup chicken broth
2½ pounds veal cut in 2-inch cubes	

Mix together the flour, salt, and pepper; roll the meat in the mixture.

Melt the butter in a casserole; brown the meat on all sides. Arrange the endive around the meat and add ½ cup of the broth. Cover and bake in a 325° oven 2 hours, basting frequently and adding broth as needed. Taste for seasoning and serve with sautéed potatoes.   Serves 6.

VEAL ROULADES

6 slices veal cutlet (about 2 pounds)	1½ teaspoons salt
6 slices Swiss cheese	½ teaspoon pepper
6 paper-thin slices prosciutto or smoked ham	2 eggs, beaten
½ cup flour	¾ cup dry bread crumbs
	6 tablespoons butter

Pound the veal very thin; cut the cheese a little smaller than the meat. Place over the veal and cover with the ham. Roll up and fasten with toothpicks or thread, if necessary. Roll in the flour seasoned with salt and pepper. Dip in the eggs and then in the bread crumbs.

Melt the butter in a skillet and sauté the rolls over low heat until browned on all sides. Serves 6.

STUFFED SHOULDER OF VEAL

5-pound shoulder of veal	2 cloves garlic, minced
2 teaspoons salt	3 tablespoons salad oil
½ teaspoon pepper	2 onions, sliced
12 anchovy fillets, undrained and shredded	1 can (8 ounce) tomato sauce
	1 bay leaf
½ cup sliced black olives	½ teaspoon thyme
1 cup dry bread crumbs	

Have the veal boned and a pocket made for stuffing. Season with salt and pepper.

Mix together the anchovies, olives, bread crumbs, and garlic. Fill the pocket and tie securely with thread. Brush with the oil and place in a shallow roasting pan. Arrange the onions around the meat and add the tomato sauce, bay leaf, and thyme.

Roast in a 325° oven 3 hours, or until tender. Baste frequently and add water if pan becomes dry. Serves 6–8.

BAKED SPARERIBS WITH SAUERKRAUT

2 racks of spareribs	2 teaspoons paprika
1 tablespoon salt	2 tablespoons salad oil
¾ teaspoon pepper	2 pounds sauerkraut
½ teaspoon thyme	3 onions, sliced

Have the ribs cut in serving-size pieces. Season with a mixture of the salt, pepper, thyme, and paprika.

Spread the sauerkraut in an oiled roasting pan and arrange the onions and ribs on top. Roast in a 350° oven 1½ hours, or until tender and browned. Turn the ribs after the first half hour. Serves 6.

STUFFED HAM STEAKS (*Rebanades de Jamon*)

½ cup minced onions	¼ cup beef broth
3 tablespoons butter	2 slices ham, 1 inch thick
3 cups soft bread crumbs	1 tablespoon cornstarch
¾ cup seedless raisins	¾ cup orange juice
¼ teaspoon salt	2 tablespoons lemon juice
¼ teaspoon marjoram	¼ cup water
Dash cayenne pepper	¼ cup brown sugar

Sauté the onions in the butter 10 minutes. Add the bread crumbs, ½ cup raisins, the salt, marjoram, cayenne, and broth. Spread on 1 slice ham and cover with the other. Tie or fasten with skewers. Place in a baking pan.

Bake in a 350° oven 30 minutes. Mix the cornstarch with a little orange juice until smooth and then combine with the remaining orange juice and the lemon juice, water, brown sugar, and remaining raisins. Pour over the ham and bake 30 minutes longer, basting frequently; cut crosswise. Serves 6.

BAKED STUFFED PORK CHOPS

4 loin pork chops, 2 inches thick	1½ cups dry bread crumbs
2 teaspoons salt	2 tablespoons minced parsley
½ teaspoon pepper	⅛ teaspoon thyme
¾ cup minced onions	1 egg, beaten
2 tablespoons butter	1 tablespoon oil
¾ cup chopped mushrooms	½ cup beef broth

Have a pocket cut in each chop. Season with 1½ teaspoons salt and ¼ teaspoon pepper.

Sauté the onions in the butter 5 minutes. Add the mushrooms and sauté 5 minutes longer. Remove from the heat and stir in the bread crumbs, parsley, thyme, and egg. Stuff the chops and fasten with toothpicks or skewers.

Arrange the chops in an oiled, shallow baking pan. Bake in a 350° oven 1 hour. Turn the chops after 30 minutes and add the broth. Baste frequently. Serve with applesauce or apple fritters.

Serves 4.

FRANKFURTER ROAST

½ cup sliced onions	3 eggs, beaten
½ pound spinach, washed and drained	1 teaspoon Worcestershire sauce
2 cups sliced carrots	1½ teaspoons salt
1 cup diced green pepper	½ teaspoon freshly ground
¼ pound mushrooms	black pepper
1 cup shredded cabbage	¼ teaspoon thyme
4 tablespoons butter	12 thick frankfurters (knock-
1¼ cups dry bread crumbs	wurst)

Using the medium blade of a food chopper, grind the onions, spinach, carrots, green pepper, mushrooms, and cabbage. Sauté the mixture in butter 10 minutes, stirring frequently. Cool for 5 minutes and stir in the bread crumbs, eggs, Worcestershire sauce, salt, pepper, and thyme.

Heap in a mound on a baking pan and arrange the frankfurters around it in an upright position. (Hold in place with toothpicks.)

Bake in a 325° oven 35 minutes. Carefully transfer to a heated serving platter, using broad spatulas. The finished dish should resemble a stuffed crown roast. Serve with barbecue sauce.

Serves 6, or as many as 12.

SKEWERS OF PORK (*Satés*)

2 cups minced onions	1 tablespoon molasses
2 cloves garlic, minced	2 tablespoons lemon juice
½ cup ground Brazil nuts	4 tablespoons soy sauce
2 teaspoons salt	1½ pounds pork cut in 1-inch
½ teaspoon dried, ground chili	cubes
peppers	3 tablespoons oil
2 teaspoons ground coriander	

Pound together the onions, garlic, nuts, salt, chili peppers, and coriander. Blend in the molasses, lemon juice, and soy sauce. Toss the meat in this mixture until well coated. Set aside for 1 hour.

Thread the meat on 6 small skewers. Brush with oil. Broil 5 inches from the heat until browned, turning the skewers frequently to permit pork to cook through.

Serves 6.

Note: For hors d'oeuvre, cut the pork in ½-inch cubes and use small wooden or metal skewers.

FRANKFURTER-BEAN CASSEROLE

1½ cups dried kidney beans	½ teaspoon freshly ground
¼ cup olive oil	black pepper
2 cups minced onions	½ teaspoon orégano
1 clove garlic	½ teaspoon ground cumin seed
2½ cups canned tomatoes,	1½ pounds beef frankfurters
drained	cut in 2-inch pieces
2½ teaspoons salt	

Wash the beans and soak overnight in water to cover. Drain. Add fresh water to cover and 1 tablespoon oil. Bring to a boil and cook over low heat until beans are almost tender, about 1½ hours. Drain.

Heat the remaining oil in a casserole; sauté the onions and

garlic 15 minutes, stirring frequently. Add the tomatoes, salt, pepper, orégano, and cumin seed. Cook over low heat 15 minutes. Add the beans and frankfurters. Cover and cook 30 minutes. Taste for seasoning.

Serves 6–8.

BARBECUED FRANKFURTERS

¼ cup minced onions	2 teaspoons Worcestershire
2 tablespoons salad oil	sauce
¾ cup chili sauce	1½ teaspoons chili powder
¾ cup water	⅛ teaspoon Tabasco
½ teaspoon salt	12 frankfurters
1 teaspoon sugar	

Sauté the onions in the oil 10 minutes; stir in the chili sauce, water, salt, sugar, Worcestershire sauce, chili powder, and Tabasco. Cook over low heat 20 minutes. Add the frankfurters and cook 15 minutes, turning them frequently.

Serve on frankfurter rolls or on plates with beans.

Serves 6–12.

KIDNEYS, NEW ORLEANS STYLE

3 beef kidneys	¾ cup sliced stuffed green
4 tablespoons flour	olives
2 teaspoons salt	1 bay leaf
½ teaspoon pepper	⅛ teaspoon thyme
4 slices bacon, minced	2 tablespoons minced parsley
1 clove garlic, minced	2 cups canned tomatoes
1 cup minced onions	
1 cup thinly sliced green	
peppers	

Wash, split, and remove the core from each kidney. Cover with salted water and let soak 15 minutes. Drain. Add fresh water to cover and bring to a boil. Cook 3 minutes. Drain and cut into ½-inch slices. Sprinkle with a mixture of the flour, 1 teaspoon salt, and ¼ teaspoon pepper.

In a deep skillet, half-cook the bacon. Add the kidneys and brown on both sides. Add the garlic, onions, green peppers, and remaining salt and pepper. Sauté 5 minutes. Stir in the olives, bay leaf, thyme, parsley, and tomatoes. Cover and cook over low heat 30 minutes, or until kidneys are tender. Taste for seasoning; discard bay leaf. Serve with rice.

Serves 6.

CHEESE AND EGGS

CHEESE-EGGS

4 tablespoons butter	1 teaspoon salt
4 slices bread, trimmed	¼ teaspoon pepper
4 slices American cheese	½ cup grated American cheese
4 eggs	¼ cup heavy cream

Preheat oven to 375°.

Melt the butter in a skillet that has an ovenproof handle. Arrange the bread in the skillet and brown the underside. Remove from heat. Turn the bread over and place a piece of cheese on each slice. Carefully break an egg on each and sprinkle with salt, pepper, and grated cheese. Pour the cream over all.

Bake 10 minutes, or until the eggs are set.

Serves 2–4.

CHEESE CHILI (*Chili con Queso*)

½ cup minced onion	½ teaspoon salt
1 tablespoon olive oil	1 tablespoon chili powder
1 cup canned tomatoes, well drained	1 cup grated American or Cheddar cheese
½ cup light cream	2 eggs, beaten

Sauté the onion in the olive oil 10 minutes, stirring frequently. Add the tomatoes, cream, salt, and chili powder; cover and cook over low heat 15 minutes. Stir in the cheese until melted, then gradually beat in the eggs. Cook, stirring constantly, until thickened, but do not let boil.

Serve on toast.

Serves 4.

CHEESE RAMEKINS

8 slices white bread
8 slices Swiss cheese
3 eggs
1 cup milk

1 cup light cream
1 teaspoon salt
⅛ teaspoon nutmeg

Preheat oven to 375°.

Trim the bread and cut each slice in half. Cut the cheese the same size as the bread. In a buttered baking dish arrange the bread and cheese in an overlapping design.

Beat together the eggs, milk, cream, salt, and nutmeg. Pour over the cheese and bread. Set baking dish in a pan containing 1 inch of hot water. Bake 30 minutes, or until set and browned.

Serves 6.

PIPERADE

½ cup thinly sliced green
  pepper
½ cup thinly sliced green
  onions
1 clove garlic, minced
3 tablespoons olive oil
½ cup diced tomatoes

1 teaspoon salt
¼ teaspoon freshly ground
  black pepper
¼ cup finely chopped ham
2 tablespoons butter
4 eggs, beaten

Sauté the green pepper, onions, and garlic in the olive oil 5 minutes. Add the tomatoes, salt, and pepper. Cook over low heat 10 minutes, stirring frequently. Add the ham and cook 10 minutes longer. Add the butter and let melt; pour the eggs over all and cook until set, stirring 3 times. The result is like a scrambled omelet. Serves 2.

SWISS CHEESE AND TOMATO TART

4 tablespoons butter	½ teaspoon paprika
2 tablespoons flour	¼ teaspoon nutmeg
1 cup milk	1 cup grated Swiss cheese
1 cup heavy cream	9-inch baked pie shell
6 egg yolks	Sliced tomatoes
½ teaspoon salt	

Melt the butter in a saucepan; stir in the flour. Gradually add the milk and cream, stirring constantly to the boiling point. Cook over low heat 5 minutes.

Beat the egg yolks, salt, paprika, and nutmeg in a bowl. Gradually add the white sauce, stirring steadily to prevent curdling. Return to the saucepan and add the cheese. Cook over low heat, stirring steadily until mixture thickens. Cool and pour into the pie shell.

Just before serving, arrange sliced tomatoes in an overlapping design around the edge of the pie plate. Delicious as a luncheon or late-supper dish.

Serves 6–8.

ITALIAN FRIED CHEESE (*Mozzarella in Carozza*)

You may prepare as many carozzas as you need. Cut 3-inch rounds or squares of bread. Cover with pieces of Mozzarella cheese the same size. Dip each piece in flour seasoned with salt and pepper, and then in beaten egg.

Fry in a mixture of hot olive oil and butter until delicately browned. Serve hot.

CHEESE-ANCHOVY BREAD (*Spiedini alla Romana*)

1 loaf unsliced white bread	¼ pound butter, softened
Mozzarella (or American) cheese	½ cup minced anchovies

Trim the crusts from the unsliced bread. Cut in half lengthwise and then cut each half in thirds, crosswise. You should now have 6 pieces measuring approximately 2 inches by 5. Slice each piece crosswise at ½-inch intervals but not all the way to the bottom. Insert a thin slice of cheese in each cut and brush all over with butter. Arrange the loaves on a buttered baking sheet and sprinkle with anchovies.

Bake in a 450° oven 10 minutes, or until browned. Serve hot. Serves 6.

SANDWICHES

FRANKFURTERS IN BLANKETS

1. Split frankfurter rolls and spread with mustard. Place a cooked frankfurter in each roll and cover with 2 or 3 tablespoons of grated Cheddar cheese. Bake in a 425° oven 5 minutes, or until cheese melts.

2. Toast frankfurter rolls and place a grilled frankfurter in each. Cover with hot chili con carne (homemade or canned) and serve with finely minced onion.

3. Toast frankfurter rolls and spread with mustard. Place a grilled frankfurter in each and heap with hot sauerkraut.

4. Wrap a strip of bacon around each frankfurter and broil until bacon is crisp. Serve on toasted frankfurter rolls with mustard and relish.

FRENCH-FRIED CHEESE SANDWICHES
(Croque-Monsieur)

¾ cup grated Swiss cheese	4 slices ham
3 tablespoons heavy cream	2 eggs
8 thin slices white bread, trimmed	1½ teaspoons salt
	6 tablespoons butter

Mix the cheese and cream together. Spread the mixture on 4 slices of bread and place a slice of ham over each. Cover with remaining bread.

Beat the eggs and salt together; dip the sandwiches in the eggs. Fry in hot butter until browned on both sides. Serve hot.

Note: Cut the sandwiches in 4 before dipping them in the eggs—they'll make delicious hors d'oeuvre.

* * *

WHY DO YOU "TOAST" SOMEONE?

The wassail bowl was the classic drink for the Christmas to New Year's week in medieval England. Slices of toasted bread were always a part of the wassail bowl, for nourishment and decoration. It was customary to drink to the good health of all those present; soon these wishes were referred to as "toasts."

During the eighteenth century so many wishes of good health were offered to the most popular ladies of their day that they were said to be "the toasts of the season." Even today the person who presides at a banquet is called the "toastmaster" in honor of his ancient right to propose wishes for the good health, the toasts, of distinguished guests.

* * *

FRENCH-FRIED MUSHROOM AND HAM SANDWICH

½ lb. mushrooms	1 teaspoon salt
¼ pound ham	⅛ teaspoon pepper
3 tablespoons butter	⅛ teaspoon nutmeg
8 slices white bread	1½ cups milk
2 eggs	Fat for frying

Chop the mushrooms and ham; sauté in the butter 5 minutes. Spread on 4 slices of bread and cover with remaining slices.

Beat the eggs, salt, pepper, and nutmeg together. Dip the sandwiches in the milk and then in the egg mixture.

In a skillet, heat 2 inches of fat to 370° and fry the sandwiches until delicately browned on both sides. Drain and serve hot.

PIZZA SANDWICHES

12 thin slices bread, trimmed	½ teaspoon orégano
6 slices Mozzarella cheese	½ teaspoon freshly ground
12 anchovies	black pepper
12 slices tomato	½ cup olive oil

Toast one side of the bread. On the toasted side of 6 slices, place a piece of Mozzarella, 2 anchovies, and 2 slices tomato sprinkled with orégano and pepper. Cover with the remaining bread, toasted side down. Press the edges together.

Heat the oil in a skillet and sauté the sandwiches until browned on both sides.

Note: Smaller versions make excellent hot hors d'oeuvre—cut the bread in half or quarters.

WESTERN SANDWICH

1 tablespoon salad oil	2 eggs
¼ cup chopped onion	½ teaspoon salt
2 tablespoons chopped green pepper	⅛ teaspoon pepper
¼ cup diced ham	4 slices buttered toast

Heat half the oil in an 8-inch skillet; sauté the onion and green pepper 5 minutes. Add the ham and sauté 5 minutes longer. Beat the eggs, salt, and pepper together. Add remaining oil to the skillet and heat. Pour the eggs over all, mix lightly once, and cook over low heat until lightly browned on underside. Turn carefully and brown other side.

Cut in half and place between the toast. Serve with ketchup and pickles.

Serves 2.

NIÇOISE SANDWICH (*Pan Bagnat*)

You may use any proportions you like. Cut French bread in 6-inch lengths and split. Sprinkle the bread with olive oil. Arrange sliced onions, thinly sliced green pepper, Italian or Greek black olives, and anchovy fillets on half of the bread. Sprinkle with freshly ground black pepper, a little wine vinegar, and olive oil. Cover with remaining bread and let stand awhile to mellow.

WISCONSIN TURKEY SANDWICHES

2 tablespoons butter	1½ cups grated cheddar cheese
2 tablespoons flour	4 slices toast
¾ teaspoon salt	8 slices cooked turkey
⅛ teaspoon dry mustard	4 thin slices cooked ham
1½ cups milk	

Melt the butter in a saucepan; blend in the flour, salt, and mustard. Gradually add the milk, stirring constantly to the boiling point. Cook over low heat 5 minutes. Add the cheese, stirring until it melts.

Arrange the toast in a buttered baking pan with 2 slices of turkey on each. Pour cheese sauce over the turkey. Bake in a 450° oven 10 minutes.

Fry the ham until browned and crisp and place on top of each sandwich.

Serve hot.

FARM TOAST

8 slices bacon   8 slices apple

4 slices bread   4 slices American cheese

Fry the bacon until half cooked. Remove from pan. Lightly brown the bread in the bacon fat. Remove. Cook the apples in the bacon fat until tender but firm.

Place 2 slices of apple on each piece of bread and top with cheese and bacon. Broil in hot oven until cheese melts.

TOASTED CHEESE BREAD

Use a French bread and cut at 1-inch intervals, but not through the bottom. Butter all cut surfaces and sprinkle generously with Parmesan cheese.

Bake in a 350° oven 5–10 minutes, or until browned.

DESSERTS

The following desserts, delicious alone, are even better when served with beer.

APPLE-CHEESE PIE

Pastry for 2-crust pie
¾ cup sugar
2 tablespoons flour
⅛ teaspoon salt
1 cup (¼ pound) grated
American cheese

5 cups sliced tart apples
1 teaspoon lemon juice
3 tablespoons heavy cream

Preheat oven to 425°.

Line a 9-inch pie plate with half the pastry. Mix together the sugar, flour, salt, and cheese. Spread half the mixture on the pastry and cover with the apples mixed with the lemon juice. Spread remaining cheese mixture over the apples and pour the cream over all. Roll out remaining pastry and cover the pie. Make a few gashes on top. Brush with cream.

Bake 45 minutes, or until browned.

Delicious hot or cold.

* * *

Until the nineteenth century, beer could not be brewed during the summer months because of the hot weather. It was a German, von Linde, who perfected the refrigeration process that permitted beer to be made all year round.

APPLE PIE WITH CHEESE CRUST

2¼ cups sifted flour	6 cups sliced tart apples
½ teaspoon salt	⅔ cup sugar
¾ cup shortening	2 teaspoons lemon juice
¾ cup grated American cheese	½ teaspoon cinnamon
⅓ cup ice water	1 tablespoon butter

Sift the flour and salt into a bowl; cut in the shortening with a pastry blender or 2 knives until the consistency of corn meal. Cut in the cheese. Add 1 tablespoon of ice water at a time, tossing lightly until balls of dough are formed. Use only as much of the water as necessary to make the particles adhere. Press together in a ball; wrap in waxed paper and chill 30 minutes. Set oven at 425°.

Roll out half the dough to fit a 9-inch pie plate. Toss together the apples, sugar, lemon juice, and cinnamon. Heap in the prepared pie plate and dot with the butter. Roll out remaining dough and cover the apples. Seal pastry. Make a few gashes on the top and brush with beaten egg yolk, cream, or melted butter.

Bake 45 minutes, or until browned. Serve warm or at room temperature.

Unusual Recipes and Party Ideas

GAME RECIPES

In early colonial days the Pilgrims depended on game found abundantly in the forests. They prepared it in many ways, frequently using beer as a marinade to flavor it. Of course they drank beer when eating game, for it was their favorite beverage.

Today the game that our forefathers took for granted has become the gourmet's choice for special and festive occasions. Whether you have a hunter in the family who keeps you supplied with game or whether you buy it at the local butcher's, game offers a rare treat. Prepare it in one of the ways suggested in this section and serve it with sparkling ale or beer. Inasmuch as game is more plentiful in the fall of the year, you can continue the seasonal theme in your table decorations. Use brightly colored leaves, gourds, apples, pears, and cranberries either in appropriate containers or artistically arranged on the tablecloth. Chill the ale or beer in wooden buckets, a cooler, or pottery bowl.

*   *   *

I wish you a merry Christmass and a happy New Year
With your pockets full of money and your cellar full
of beer.
—Old English Christmas Carol

HASENPFEFFER

2 2-pound rabbits	2 teaspoons salt
¾ cup cider vinegar	¼ teaspoon pepper
1½ cups beer	½ cup flour
½ cup grated onion	4 tablespoons butter
1 tablespoon mixed pickling spice	1 cup thinly sliced onions
	1 tablespoon sugar

Have the rabbit cut in serving pieces. Wash and soak the meat in salted water 1 hour. Drain.

In a bowl (not metal) combine the vinegar, beer, grated onion, pickling spice, salt, and pepper. Mix well and add the rabbit. Let marinate 36–48 hours. Remove the rabbit and dry with paper towels. Strain the marinade and reserve. Roll the meat in the flour.

Melt the butter in a casserole or deep skillet; brown the rabbit and sliced onions. Pour off the fat and add 1½ cups marinade and the sugar. Cover and cook over low heat 1½ hours, or until the rabbit is tender. Add more marinade if needed. Delicious with dumplings. Serves 6–8.

RABBIT IN ALE SAUCE

1 2- to 3-pound rabbit	2 tablespoons prepared mustard
1 tablespoon vinegar	2 slices bread, cubed
6 slices bacon, chopped	1½ cups ale or beer
1½ cups thinly sliced onions	1 teaspoon sugar
2 teaspoons salt	2 tablespoons minced parsley
½ teaspoon freshly ground black pepper	

Have the rabbit cut in serving pieces. Cover with water and add the vinegar; let soak 1 hour. Drain and dry.

Fry the bacon in a casserole and remove. Drain all but 3 tablespoons fat and brown the onions. Remove the onions and brown the rabbit. Return the onions and sprinkle with the salt and pepper. Toss the mustard and bread cubes together and add to the casserole with the bacon, ale, and sugar. Cover tightly.

Bake in a 325° oven 2 hours, or until rabbit is tender. Sprinkle with parsley.

Serves 3–4.

* * *

Rameses III, Pharaoh of Egypt, once offered over twenty-five thousand gallons of beer to conciliate the gods.

SWEET AND SOUR RABBIT

1 2-pound rabbit	3 tablespoons lemon juice
2 tablespoons vinegar	½ cup canned tomato sauce
⅓ cup olive or salad oil	1 cup beef broth
1 onion, minced	2 tablespoons molasses
1 clove garlic, minced	¼ cup seedless raisins
2 teaspoons salt	¼ cup sliced blanched
¼ teaspoon pepper	almonds

Have the rabbit cut in serving pieces. Cover with water and add the vinegar. Let soak 1 hour. Drain and dry.

Heat the oil in a Dutch oven or heavy saucepan. Brown the rabbit, onion, and garlic very well. Add the salt, pepper, lemon juice, tomato sauce, broth, and molasses. Cover and cook over low heat 45 minutes, or until rabbit is tender. Add the raisins and almonds. Taste for seasoning and serve with noodles or rice.
Serves 4.

VENISON, BRUGES STYLE

¼ cup wine vinegar	1 bay leaf
2 cups beer or ale	¼ teaspoon orégano
1 cup minced onion	¼ teaspoon thyme
2 cloves garlic, minced	3 pounds venison cut in 1½-
1½ teaspoons salt	inch cubes
½ teaspoon freshly ground	4 tablespoons olive oil
black pepper	2 cups canned tomatoes

Combine the vinegar, beer, onion, garlic, salt, pepper, bay leaf, orégano, and thyme in a bowl (not metal). Add the venison and let marinate 12–24 hours or overnight in the refrigerator, basting frequently. Drain, reserving the marinade.

Heat the oil in a Dutch oven or casserole and brown the meat. Add the marinade and tomatoes. Cover and cook over low heat 1½ hours, or until tender. Thicken the gravy if necessary with 1 tablespoon potato flour mixed with a little water.   Serves 6.

VENISON RAGOUT

3 pounds venison	5 juniper berries, crushed
2 cups beer	(optional)
½ cup olive or salad oil	1 bay leaf
3 tablespoons lemon juice	2 tablespoons butter
2 cloves garlic, minced	3 onions, sliced
1 teaspoon salt	2 carrots, sliced
¾ teaspoon freshly ground	2 tablespoons flour
black pepper	

Have the venison larded. In a large bowl (not metal) combine the beer, oil, lemon juice, garlic, salt, pepper, juniper berries, and bay leaf. Mix well and add the venison. Let marinate in the refrigerator 24–36 hours.

Melt the butter in a Dutch oven or heavy skillet; sauté the onions and carrots 15 minutes, stirring frequently. Stir in the flour and then add the marinade, mixing steadily to the boiling point. Add the venison. Cover and cook over low heat 2½ hours, or until meat is tender, turning it frequently. Taste for seasoning. Discard bay leaf. Slice the meat and force the gravy through a sieve.

Serves 6–8.

VENISON SAUTÉ À LA FORESTIÈRE

½ cup wine vinegar
¾ cup olive oil
2 teaspoons salt
2 cloves garlic, minced
3 pounds loin of venison, boned
¼ cup flour
½ cup beer
1½ cups beef broth

4 crushed juniper berries (optional)
½ teaspoon thyme
¼ teaspoon savory
3 tablespoons minced parsley
2 tablespoons tomato paste
½ pound mushrooms, sliced
½ cup minced onion
2 tablespoons butter

Combine the vinegar, ½ cup olive oil, the salt and garlic in a bowl (not metal). Marinate the venison in the mixture overnight in the refrigerator. Drain the meat and dry it with paper towels.

Heat the remaining oil in a Dutch oven or heavy saucepan until it smokes. Sear the meat in it; sprinkle with the flour and let brown. Add the wine, broth, juniper berries, thyme, savory, parsley, and tomato paste. Cover and cook over low heat 2 hours.

Sauté the mushrooms and onion in the butter 10 minutes. Add to the meat. Cook 30 minutes longer, or until meat is tender.

Serves 6.

WILD DUCK, CHINESE STYLE

2 2-pound wild ducks

2 cloves garlic, minced

1 tablespoon salt

½ teaspoon freshly ground black pepper

¼ cup melted butter

1 apple, halved

¼ cup dry mustard

½ cup beer

2 tablespoons soy sauce

1 cup apricot preserves

1 tablespoon lemon juice

Clean, wash, and dry the ducks. Mix to a paste the garlic, salt, and pepper; rub into the ducks and brush the breasts heavily with butter. Place a half apple in each duck. Arrange the ducks in a shallow roasting pan, breasts up. Roast in a 400° oven 15 minutes.

Mix together the mustard, beer, soy sauce, apricot preserves, and lemon juice. Reduce the heat to 350°. Pour the sauce over the ducks and roast 30 minutes longer, basting frequently.

Serves 4.

Note: Domestic duck may be prepared in the same manner, but roast 2–2½ hours.

STUFFED GROUSE

3 tablespoons butter

2 cups finely shredded cabbage

2 cups thinly sliced onions

3 tablespoons dry bread crumbs

3 teaspoons salt

¾ teaspoon freshly ground black pepper

2 1½ pound grouse

4 slices bacon

Melt the butter in a skillet; sauté the cabbage and onions 10 minutes without browning. Stir in the bread crumbs, 1 teaspoon salt, and ¼ teaspoon pepper.

Clean, wash, and dry the grouse; season with the remaining salt and pepper. Stuff with the cabbage mixture, closing the opening with skewers, thread, or aluminum foil. Arrange in a shallow baking pan, breast side up. Place 2 slices of bacon on each. Roast in a 350° oven 40 minutes, or until tender. Baste frequently.

Serves 4.

PARTRIDGE A LA TITANIA

4 partridges	½ cup chicken broth
1 tablespoon salt	½ cup orange juice
½ teaspoon freshly ground	2 tablespoons currant jelly
black pepper	2 oranges, peeled and
5 tablespoons butter	segmented
1 tablespoon cornstarch	½ cup seedless grapes

Clean, wash, and dry the partridges; season with the salt and pepper. Melt the butter in a casserole and brown the birds on all sides. Mix the cornstarch and broth together and add to the casserole with the orange juice, jelly, oranges, and grapes. Cover tightly.

Bake in a 400° oven 25 minutes, or until tender. Taste for seasoning.

Serves 4.

PARTRIDGES, CATALANA STYLE (*Perdrices à la Catalana*)

4 partridges	2 cloves garlic, minced
2 teaspoons salt	¼ teaspoon thyme
½ teaspoon pepper	1 bay leaf
2 cups minced onions	½ square (½ ounce) unsweet-
¼ pound ground veal	ened chocolate, grated
2 tablespoons butter	¾ cup beef stock
1 cup sliced Spanish sausage	½ cup chicken broth
3 tablespoons olive oil	

Clean, wash, and dry the partridges. Season with the salt and pepper.

Sauté 1 cup onions and the veal in the butter 15 minutes, stirring frequently. Add the sausage and cook over low heat 10 minutes. Taste for seasoning and stuff the birds.

Heat the oil in a casserole or Dutch oven and brown the

partridges. Add the garlic and remaining onions and continue browning. Add the thyme, bay leaf, chocolate, stock, and broth. Cover.

Bake in a 375° oven 45 minutes, or until partridges are tender. Remove cover for last 10 minutes. Don't worry about the chocolate; you can't taste it.

Serves 4.

*   *   *

The great Emperor Charlemagne personally supervised the study and training of all brewers in his kingdom.

PHEASANT WITH SAUERKRAUT

1 pheasant, cut in half	1 cup grated potatoes
3 teaspoons salt	6 juniper berries (optional)
¾ teaspoon freshly ground black pepper	½ teaspoon caraway seeds
	2 cups chicken broth
2 pounds sauerkraut, drained	1 cup sour cream
½ cup diced onion	4 tablespoons butter

Clean, wash, and dry the pheasant; season with 2 teaspoons salt and ½ teaspoon pepper.

Combine the sauerkraut, onion, potatoes, juniper berries, caraway seeds, broth, sour cream, and remaining salt and pepper in a Dutch oven or casserole. Cover and cook over low heat 1 hour.

Brown the pheasant in the butter and place over the sauerkraut. Cover. Bake in a 350° oven 45 minutes, or until pheasant is tender. Serves 2–4.

ROAST PHEASANT WITH CHESTNUTS

1 3-pound pheasant	2 tablespoons flour
2½ teaspoons salt	1 cup chicken broth
¼ teaspoon pepper	½ cup orange juice
2 tablespoons butter	1 tablespoon currant jelly
1 tablespoon olive oil	1 bay leaf
12 small white onions	¼ teaspoon thyme
2 cups shelled chestnuts	

Clean, wash, and dry the pheasant; season with the salt and pepper.

Heat the butter and oil in a casserole; brown the pheasant on all sides. Add the onions and chestnuts and cook over low heat until lightly browned. Sprinkle with the flour and add the broth, stirring gently to the boiling point. Add the orange juice, currant jelly, bay leaf, and thyme. Cover tightly.

Roast in a 350° oven 1½ hours, basting frequently. Taste for seasoning. Discard the bay leaf. Serve with braised celery.

Serves 4.

QUAIL VERONIQUE

4 quail	4 tablespoons butter
2 teaspoons salt	½ cup chicken broth
½ teaspoon pepper	½ cup seedless green grapes
2 tablespoons flour	3 tablespoons sliced Brazil nuts

Clean, wash, and dry the quail. Rub with a mixture of the salt, pepper, and flour. Melt the butter in a deep skillet and brown the quail on all sides. Add the broth. Cover and cook over low heat 15 minutes, or until tender. Add the grapes and nuts; cook 3 minutes longer. Taste for seasoning. Serve on a slice of bread sautéed in butter.

Serves 4.

SPICED PIGEONS

2 pigeons	1 cup tarragon vinegar
2 teaspoons salt	1 cup chicken broth
½ teaspoon freshly ground black pepper	¼ teaspoon ground ginger
	10 peppercorns
4 tablespoons olive oil	2 bay leaves
1 cup thinly sliced onions	1 teaspoon sugar
2 cloves garlic, minced	

Clean the pigeons; wash and dry. Cut in half. Season with the salt and pepper. Finely mince the giblets.

Brown the pigeons in the oil. Add the onions and garlic and brown. Stir in the minced giblets, vinegar, broth, ginger, peppercorns, bay leaves, and sugar. Cover and cook over low heat 30 minutes, or until tender. Taste for seasoning. Discard bay leaf. Chill 24 hours before serving with olives, diced cream cheese, and lettuce.

Serves 4.

CASSEROLE OF PIGEONS

4 pigeons	12 scallions (green onions)
6 slices bacon	6 carrots, scraped and quartered
3 tablespoons butter	

4 potatoes, peeled and   ½ teaspoon freshly ground
  quartered   black pepper
2 cups shelled green peas or   ½ teaspoon dried thyme
  1 package frozen, thawed   ½ cup hot chicken broth
2 teaspoons salt

Buy young pigeons; clean and truss. Cover the bacon with water; bring to a boil and cook 1 minute. Drain and chop coarsely.

Melt the butter in a casserole and brown the pigeons over low heat. Remove. Add the bacon, scallions, carrots, and potatoes. Cook, shaking the casserole frequently until vegetables are delicately browned. Return the pigeons to the casserole with the peas, salt, pepper, thyme, and broth. Cover tightly. Bake in a 325° oven 1 hour, or until the pigeons are tender.

Serves 4.

PIGEON PROVENÇAL

4 pigeons   4 slices bacon, minced
1 tablespoon salt   ½ cup diced onions
½ teaspoon freshly ground   ¼ pound mushrooms, sliced
  black pepper   1 29-ounce can tomatoes,
2 cloves garlic, minced   drained
4 small white onions   ½ teaspoon thyme
8 sprigs parsley

Clean, wash, and dry the pigeons. Season with a mixture of the salt, pepper, and garlic. Place an onion and 2 sprigs of parsley inside each.

Cook the bacon slightly in a casserole or Dutch oven. Brown the pigeons in the bacon fat over high heat. Add the onions and mushrooms and continue browning 5 minutes. Add the tomatoes and thyme. Cover.

Bake in a 350° oven 1¼ hours, or until pigeons are tender. Serves 4.

AN INDIAN DINNER

Indian cooking is elaborate but, at the same time, simple to prepare. Spices are all important, but unfortunately in the United States we think of all Indian dishes as "curry," usually a cream sauce flavored with commercially prepared curry powder. Actually Indian cookery is exceedingly subtle. Each Indian family prepares its own blend of spices and each dish is flavored differently. Rice and *ghee* (clarified butter) play important roles, as well as seafood and yogurt. Cleanliness is almost a fetish in the homes of the well-born, and there is an almost ritualistic ceremony about the washing of hands before meals.

In French cooking one is taught not to use more than one or two herbs in any dish—discard this idea when cooking Indian dishes. Many herbs and spices, carefully and judiciously added, produce succulent concoctions that tempt and tease the palate.

It's exciting to entertain Indian-fashion and it's particularly adaptable for lap or living-room service. Have a round tray (*thāli*) for each person and on it arrange one large bowl for the main dish, surrounded by several small bowls containing the rice and *sambals* (accompaniments). The foods are usually cut up, thus not requiring a knife; a spoon and fork are sufficient. If you have a large cocktail table, arrange large pillows or hassocks around it and have your guests sit on them, using the table for dining. If not, the trays themselves may be kept on the lap.

If you like, a large chafing dish may be used for serving. On no account serve rice as a border or base with a curry (unless it was cooked in the sauce). It's not necessary to serve a separate salad course, as crisp vegetables are usually included in the accompaniments. Ale and beer are ideal as beverages—they both sharpen the taste of the food and quench the thirst. Chapatties (unleavened bread) are usually placed on the tray.

Among the sambals served are red or green chili peppers, gherkins, pickled onions, chutney, eggplant, diced cucumbers, chopped tomatoes, peanuts, coconut (ground or cut into pieces), seedless raisins, diced bananas, and any type of pickle you can think of.

Poppadams are crisp dried chips which, when fried in deep fat, puff up to three times their size and are served hot with Indian dishes. Packed in cans, they may be obtained at shops specializing in foreign foods.

Boorthas are Moslem savory dishes served with rice and usually contain vegetables. They are delicious not only with Indian dishes but also with a bland American meat or poultry dish.

In general, Indian sweets (desserts) are prepared with rice, nuts, and coconut. They are completely unlike the traditional American desserts but are interesting nevertheless. Dramatically arranged fresh fruit served on a bed of crushed ice is served after the sweet as a climax to an adventurous meal.

INDIAN BREAD (*Chapatties*)

1 cup sifted whole-wheat or white flour	⅛ teaspoon salt ½ cup water

Sift the flour and salt into a bowl. Gradually add just enough water to make a smooth, soft dough, blending with the fingers.

Divide into 8 pieces on a lightly floured surface. Flatten into circles and let stand 15 minutes. Roll out as thin as possible.

Bake on an ungreased griddle or skillet, turning frequently. Keep flat by pressing down with paper towel.

INDIAN FINGER FOODS (*Samosas*)

1¾ cups sifted flour
1 teaspoon salt
2 tablespoons melted butter

6 tablespoons yogurt
Fat for deep frying

Sift the flour and salt into a bowl; work in the butter and then the yogurt. Knead lightly until a dough is formed. Cover with a bowl and let stand for 30 minutes.

Break off small pieces of the dough and roll into 6-inch circles. Cut each circle in half. Shape into a cone and fill with one of the fillings. Fold over the open end and seal all the edges with water. Fry in 375° fat until browned. Serve hot.   Makes about 30.

MEAT FILLING

½ cup minced onions
1 tablespoon butter
½ pound ground beef
1 tomato, diced
1 teaspoon salt

⅛ teaspoon dried, ground chili peppers
1 teaspoon turmeric
1 tablespoon minced parsley
1 teaspoon grated lemon rind

Sauté the onions in the butter 5 minutes. Add the beef and cook over high heat, stirring almost steadily until browned. Add the tomato, salt, chili peppers, turmeric, and parsley. Cook over low heat 5 minutes, or until completely dry. Stir in the lemon rind. Cool and proceed as directed.

VEGETABLE FILLING

1 cup mashed potatoes
½ cup cooked or canned green peas
3 tablespoons grated onion
1 teaspoon salt

⅛ teaspoon dried, ground chili peppers
¼ teaspoon ground coriander
1 tablespoon minced parsley
2 teaspoons lemon juice

Mix all the ingredients together and proceed as directed.

Tall goblets of light, bright beer or ale are the perfect accompaniment for game dinners. (Recipe for *Quail Veronique* on page 187.)

CHICKEN KUNDOU

¼ pound butter
2 cups thinly sliced onions
2 cloves garlic, minced
2 2½-pound fryers, disjointed
2 tomatoes, chopped
2 teaspoons salt

¼ teaspoon dried, ground chili peppers
1½ teaspoons ground ginger
1½ cups sour milk or buttermilk
½ cup ground cashew nuts
½ cup heavy cream

In a casserole or Dutch oven, melt the butter. Sauté the onions and garlic 10 minutes. Add the chicken and cook until it begins to brown. Add the tomatoes, salt, chili peppers, ginger, sour milk, and nuts. Cover and cook over low heat 1 hour. Add the cream and taste for seasoning. Serve with Coconut Rice. Serves 8.

CHICKEN SUKH

1½ cups dried chick peas or 3 cups canned
2 2-pound chickens, disjointed
1 teaspoon ground ginger
2½ teaspoons salt
½ teaspoon freshly ground black pepper

4 onions, thinly sliced
4 tablespoons butter
½ teaspoon ground cumin
2 teaspoons crushed coriander
⅛ teaspoon ground cloves
1 cup chicken stock

If dried chick peas are used, wash and soak overnight in water to cover. Cook until barely tender, about 2 hours. Drain.

Wash and dry the chickens. Mix together the ginger, salt, pepper, and onions. Combine with the chicken, tossing together lightly.

Melt the butter in a casserole or Dutch oven. Turn the chicken mixture and chick peas into it and sauté until browned. Add the cumin, coriander, cloves, and stock. Cover and cook over low heat 45 minutes, or until chicken and chick peas are tender.
Serves 6–8.

DUCK, BOMBAY STYLE

4- to 5-pound duck	1½ cups finely chopped onions
2 teaspoons ground ginger	3 cloves garlic, minced
½ teaspoon saffron	¼ teaspoon dried, ground red
1½ teaspoons salt	peppers
¼ cup soy sauce	2 bay leaves
4 tablespoons peanut or salad	¾ cup water
oil	

Have the duck cut into small pieces; wash and dry it. Mix together the ginger, saffron, salt, and soy sauce; rub the mixture into the duck. Let stand at room temperature 1 hour.

Heat 1 tablespoon oil in a deep skillet and brown the duck. Remove the duck and pour off all the fat. Heat remaining oil in the skillet; sauté the onions and garlic 5 minutes. Return the duck to the skillet and add the red peppers, bay leaves, and water. Cover and cook over low heat 1 hour, or until duck is tender. Serve on a bed of rice. Serves 4–5.

COCONUT RICE

1 cup fresh or dried grated	¼ pound butter
coconut	½ cup minced onions
4 cups milk	1½ tablespoons curry powder
2 cups rice	1½ teaspoons salt

If dried coconut is used, wash under running water to remove the sweetness. Combine the coconut and milk in a saucepan; bring to a boil and let soak 30 minutes. (If you have a blender, run the coconut mixture in it until completely liquid. If not, press all the liquid from the coconut and discard the pulp.) Wash the rice in several changes of water and drain.

Melt the butter in a heavy saucepan and sauté the onions 5

minutes. Stir in the curry powder and rice. Cook over low heat, stirring almost constantly for 5 minutes. Add the coconut milk and salt. Cover and cook over low heat 15 minutes, or until rice is tender. Watch carefully and add a little boiling water if the milk is absorbed before the rice is tender. Serves 6–8.

AGRA LAMB CURRY

1 teaspoon cumin seed	1½ cups minced onions
2 teaspoons coriander seed	2 pounds leg or shoulder of
2 teaspoons turmeric	lamb cut in 2-inch pieces
1 teaspoon ground ginger	2 teaspoons salt
¼ teaspoon dried, ground chili	½ cup yogurt
peppers	½ cup chopped tomatoes
4 tablespoons butter	

Crush the cumin and coriander seeds in a mortar with pestle, or with a rolling pin between sheets of waxed paper. Mix with the turmeric, ginger, and chili peppers.

Melt the butter in a casserole or Dutch oven; sauté the onions for 20 minutes, stirring frequently. Add the lamb and spices. Cook over very low heat, stirring frequently until lamb browns. Stir in the salt, yogurt, and tomatoes. Cook until liquid is absorbed and add ½ cup water. Cover and cook over low heat 1½ hours, or until lamb is tender. Add water when necessary. Serves 4.

LENTIL CURRY (Dahl)

2 cups lentils	2 pounds lamb cut in 1½-inch
1 teaspoon cumin seed	cubes
1½ cups finely chopped onions	6 tablespoons butter
3 cloves garlic, minced	1 onion, sliced
2 teaspoons salt	8 crushed peppercorns
¼ cup yogurt	1 teaspoon turmeric

Wash the lentils, discarding any imperfect ones. Cover with water; bring to a boil. Remove from heat and let soak 1 hour. Drain.

Pound the cumin seed to a powder, then combine with the onions and garlic. Pound to a paste. Add the salt, yogurt, and lamb. Toss together and set aside 1 hour.

Melt the butter in a casserole or Dutch oven and sauté the sliced onion 10 minutes. Add the meat; cover and cook over low heat 15 minutes, shaking the casserole vigorously once or twice. Add the lentils, boiling water to cover, the peppercorns, and turmeric. Cover and cook over medium-low heat 1 hour, or until meat and lentils are tender. Most of the water should be absorbed—this is a fairly dry dish. Serves 4–6.

CUCUMBER RELISH (*Boortha*)

3 cucumbers, peeled and sliced	⅛ teaspoon dried, ground chili peppers
½ cup water	
½ cup chopped onions	½ teaspoon ground ginger
½ cup chopped green pepper	2 tablespoons olive or salad oil
½ teaspoon salt	2 tablespoons lemon juice

Cook the cucumbers in the water until soft, about 10 minutes. Drain. Chop together the cucumbers, onions, and green pepper. Add the salt, chili peppers, ginger, oil, and lemon juice. Continue chopping until very fine. Chill.

Makes about 2 cups.

CUCUMBER AND TOMATO SAMBALS

¾ cup minced onion	½ teaspoon ground ginger
2 cloves garlic, minced	1 teaspoon turmeric
4 tablespoons butter	¼ teaspoon ground cumin seed
1 teaspoon salt	2 cucumbers, thinly sliced
¼ teaspoon dried, ground chili peppers	2 tomatoes, diced

Sauté the onion and garlic in the butter 10 minutes, stirring frequently. Stir in the salt, chili peppers, ginger, turmeric, and cumin seed. Cook 2 minutes longer.

Divide the mixture and place in 2 bowls. Add the cucumbers to one and the tomatoes to the other. Mix lightly and let stand 1 hour before serving. Serve in separate bowls.

Makes about 1½ cups.

FRUIT CHUTNEY

1 pound apples, thinly sliced
½ pound prunes, diced
½ pound dried apricots, chopped
2 tablespoons seedless raisins
1½ cups brown sugar
1 cup cider vinegar
1½ teaspoons chili powder
1½ teaspoons salt
⅛ teaspoon dried, ground chili peppers
1 teaspoon cinnamon
½ teaspoon freshly ground black pepper
½ teaspoon ground cloves
½ teaspoon coriander
2 teaspoons ground ginger
3 cloves garlic, minced

Combine all the ingredients in a saucepan (not aluminum). Bring to a boil and cook over low heat 45 minutes, stirring frequently with a wooden spoon. The mixture should be soft and brown. Cool and pack into clean jars.

Makes about 1 pint.

EGGPLANT RELISH (*Brinjal Boortha*)

1 medium eggplant
4 tablespoons flaked coconut
2 tablespoons heavy cream
⅓ cup finely chopped onions
¼ cup finely chopped green pepper
1½ teaspoons salt
⅛ teaspoon dried, ground chili peppers
⅛ teaspoon dry mustard
2 tablespoons lemon juice

Loosely wrap the eggplant in aluminum foil and bake in a 375°
oven 1 hour. Cool and peel. Wash the coconut under running water
to remove the sweetness, then combine with the cream.

Chop together the eggplant, onions, green pepper, and undrained coconut. Add the salt, chili peppers, mustard, and lemon
juice. Chop until very fine. Taste for seasoning and serve cold.
Makes about 3 cups.

TOMATO CHUTNEY

4 pounds firm tomatoes	¼ teaspoon freshly ground
3 large onions	black pepper
3 tart apples, cored and sliced	1 cup dark brown sugar, packed
thin	3 tablespoons lemon juice
1 cup beer	2 tablespoons grated lemon rind
2 cups cider vinegar	¼ teaspoon powdered ginger
1½ tablespoons salt	¼ teaspoon mace

Peel the tomatoes and cut in quarters; cut the onions in half
and slice thin. Combine in a saucepan with the apples, beer, vinegar, salt, pepper, brown sugar, lemon juice, rind, ginger, and mace.

Bring to a boil and cook over low heat 1½ hours, or until thick
and browned. Turn into sterile jars and cover tightly. Serve with
curries or roast lamb.

Makes about 1½ pints.

RICE DESSERT (*Meeta Pillau*)

1½ cups raw rice	½ teaspoon salt
¼ pound butter	½ cup seedless raisins
⅛ teaspoon ground cloves	½ cup sliced, blanched, toasted
⅛ teaspoon ground allspice	almonds
1 teaspoon cinnamon	⅓ cup sugar
⅛ teaspoon saffron	

Buy long-grain rice and wash under running water for 5 minutes. Drain well.

Melt the butter in a saucepan; add the rice. Cook over low heat, stirring almost constantly until rice is delicately browned. Stir in the cloves, allspice, cinnamon, saffron, salt, and enough boiling water to cover. Cover tightly and cook over low heat until the water is absorbed. Add the raisins, nuts, and sugar. Cook 2 minutes. Serve hot.

Serves 6.

SMØRREBRØD

Smørrebrød, literally open sandwiches, are eaten by everyone in Denmark for lunch and are so much a part of their life that the custom might almost be called a cult. We might do well to borrow it—not only does it do away with an unnecessary slice of bread, but the appearance is exciting and imaginative. They're wonderful for a man's card party—easily prepared by the man of the family or a thoughtful wife. Make them beforehand, cover them with aluminum foil or waxed paper; they'll be ready to serve when needed later in the evening with chilled beer.

The varieties are endless—any combination that appeals to you may be used. If you're serving a selection, the order in the Danish fashion is fish first, then eggs, meat, and last of all, cheese.

Dark, whole-grained bread, sliced very thin, is usually the base. But white bread, toasted if you like, may also be used. Here are just a few of the combinations:

Egg and Anchovy

Arrange slices of hard-cooked eggs on buttered bread and place 2 anchovy fillets on top lengthwise. Decorate with watercress or parsley.

Herring and Tomato

Cover buttered bread with thinly sliced tomato. Arrange slices of pickled herring on top, sprinkled with a little minced onion.

Shrimp

Danish shrimp are very small and are available in cans. If you use domestic shrimp, buy the smallest ones you can find and arrange them on buttered white bread so that they completely cover the bread and come to a peak in the center. Place a teaspoonful of mayonnaise in the center and sprinkle with minced dill or parsley.

Smoked Salmon and Scrambled Eggs

Cover buttered bread with smoked salmon and arrange cold scrambled eggs diagonally across it in a 1-inch strip. Sprinkle the eggs with dill or paprika.

Lobster Salad

Place a lettuce leaf, cut to fit, on a piece of buttered bread. Heap the lobster salad on it, and place 2 cooked or canned asparagus tips on it.

Tomato and Onion

Arrange slices of tomato on heavily buttered bread. Put a dab of sour cream in the center and sprinkle with chopped onion.

Beef and Fried Egg

Cover buttered bread with thinly sliced roast beef. Cover with fried onions, and over that place a sunny-side-up egg.

Ham and Egg

Place a slice of thinly sliced boiled ham on buttered bread and heap cold scrambled eggs in the center. Sprinkle with chopped chives.

Hans Christian Andersen

Place 3 slices of crisp bacon on buttered bread. Cover one half with pâté (see recipes) and arrange sliced tomatoes on the other half.

Cold duck, chicken, steak, or pork may be used too. Slice cheese a little thicker than usual and arrange on buttered bread. Just be sure the sandwiches are attractive and served with properly chilled beer. You'll have a successful party.

* * *

The first help-wanted advertisement for work in America appeared in a London newspaper. It requested the services of experienced brewers for the Virginia colony. Two Frenchmen responded to the ad, were hired, and proved to be completely satisfactory in the New World.

A SWEDISH SMÖRGÅSBORD

The formal seated dinner of many courses has largely disappeared from the modern scene. In its place has come informal, friendly entertaining—an American innovation. One of the most pleasing and unceremonious methods of entertaining guests is the smörgåsbord. Best of all, the hostess is free to join her guests, for there is practically nothing for her to do at the last moment but to enjoy the party.

A smörgåsbord consists primarily of a dozen or more assorted appetizers, cold cuts, hot dishes, and cheese. All of these are attractively arranged on a table, and everyone helps himself. Guests take a small plate, a knife, fork, and napkin from the table and make their own selections from the various platters. The etiquette of the smörgåsbord requires that each person make three trips to the table —first for fish preparations, then for meat dishes, and finally for cheese. It is therefore nice but not necessary to have three plates for each person. The perfect drink is beer, for there is nothing that so well accompanies various flavors.

The first part of a smörgåsbord is herring and other tinned fish. Visit your local supermarket or food shop and make a selection of canned or bottled herrings, sardines, and other fish items. These should be well chilled; if desired, they may be served directly from the tin or container in the Swedish fashion, or may be appealingly arranged on platters, each with its own serving utensil. Boiled potatoes are traditionally served with herring, but be sure they are not too large or overcooked. A selection of several kinds of sliced breads and sweet butter is always a part of the smörgåsbord.

Dishes of raw vegetables (celery, carrots, turnip, cauliflowerets) on a bed of ice are always attractive. Green and black olives are appropriate additions to the classic smörgåsbord. For more elaborate parties, beet, potato, cold vegetable, or chicken salads might be prepared. A sliced tongue or ham (or both) add a substantial note to the meal, particularly for hungry men. Other suggestions might be a roast turkey or roast beef, both partially cut, with slices of meat arranged about the platter's edge. For elaborate festivities, hot dishes (such as Swedish meat balls or sweetbreads) are served in a chafing dish.

By Swedish unwritten law, there is always a large platter of assorted cheese to conclude the smörgåsbord. Be daring—buy several different (and unusual) varieties. For full flavor, the cheese should be kept at room temperature—that is, out of the refrigerator—at least 4 hours before the guests arrive. Serve the cheese with several kinds of crackers and dark, whole-grained breads and of course more cool, delightfully refreshing glasses of beer.

BAKED SWEDISH PÂTÉ (*Leverpastej*)

1½ pounds calf's liver	½ teaspoon freshly ground
¼ pound bacon	black pepper
¾ cup diced onion	¼ teaspoon nutmeg
5 anchovy fillets	¾ cup flour
2 teaspoons salt	1½ cups light cream

Using the fine blade of a food chopper, grind together 3 times the liver, bacon, onion, and anchovies. Turn into a bowl and add the salt, pepper, nutmeg, and flour. Gradually add the cream, beating all the while until light and fluffy. Turn into a greased 9-inch loaf pan. Set in a shallow pan of hot water.

Bake in a 300° oven 1½ hours, or until set. Cool thoroughly before removing from pan. Chill, slice thin, and serve with buttered bread.

Makes about 25–30 slices.

SWEDISH MEAT BALLS

¼ cup dry bread crumbs	1 egg
¼ cup cream	3 tablespoons grated onion
1 pound ground beef	2 tablespoons butter
½ pound ground pork	2 tablespoons flour
2 teaspoons salt	1½ cups beer
½ teaspoon freshly ground	3 tablespoons minced dill or
black pepper	½ teaspoon crushed dill seeds
⅛ teaspoon thyme	

Soak the bread crumbs in the cream for 5 minutes, then mix lightly with the beef, pork, 1 teaspoon salt, ¼ teaspoon pepper, thyme, egg, and onion. Shape into 1-inch balls.

Melt the butter in a skillet and brown the meat balls. Remove the meat balls and pour off all but 2 tablespoons of the fat. Stir the flour into the skillet until brown. Gradually add the beer, stirring constantly to the boiling point. Return the meat balls to the skillet; stir in the dill and remaining salt and pepper. Cover and cook over low heat 20 minutes. Taste for seasoning. Serves 6.

SWEDISH HAMBURGER PIE

6 onions, sliced	1 pound ground beef
4 tablespoons butter	1 egg
2 teaspoons sugar	1½ teaspoons salt
1 slice white bread	½ teaspoon freshly ground
½ cup beer	black pepper
½ cup mashed potato	4 tablespoons beef broth

Sauté the onions in the butter 15 minutes, stirring frequently; sprinkle with the sugar after 5 minutes.

Soak the bread in the beer, then mash fine. Combine with the potato, beef, egg, salt, and pepper. Mix very well and taste for seasoning.

Spread two thirds of the onions on the bottom of a greased 9 inch pie plate. Spread the meat over it and cover with remaining onions. Pour the broth over all.

Bake in a 400° oven 40 minutes. Serve hot, cut in wedges. Serves 6.

HOT POTATO SALAD

2 pounds small potatoes	¼ cup water
4 slices bacon, minced	½ cup cider vinegar
¼ cup minced onion	½ teaspoon sugar
¼ cup chopped green pepper	1 teaspoon salt
½ cup chopped dill pickle	¼ teaspoon dry mustard
¼ cup minced pimiento	½ teaspoon paprika

Cook the unpeeled potatoes until tender but firm, about 20 minutes. Peel and slice while hot.

Cook the bacon in a skillet until some fat melts, then stir in the onion and green pepper. Sauté for 10 minutes, stirring frequently.

Add the pickle, pimiento, water, vinegar, sugar, salt, mustard, and paprika. Bring to a boil and pour over the potatoes. Toss lightly and serve while hot. Serves 8.

SPICED PRUNES, SCANDINAVIAN STYLE

1 pound unsweetened prunes	¼ teaspoon powdered ginger
2 cups beer	½ teaspoon cinnamon
½ cup water	6 thin slices lemon
⅓ cup brown sugar	½ cup blanched almonds
1 teaspoon whole cloves	

Wash the prunes; combine in a saucepan with the beer, water, brown sugar, cloves, ginger, and cinnamon. Cover and bring to a boil; cook over low heat 20 minutes. Remove from the heat and let stand 2 hours. Add the lemon and almonds; return to heat and simmer 30 minutes longer. Serve hot or cold with meat or game. Makes about 1½ pints.

SWEDISH HAM

Precooked ham	1½ cups brown sugar
2½ cups beer	1 teaspoon dry mustard
Cloves	

You may use a whole or half ham—buy the type you prefer and follow packer's instructions for cooking it. Remove the skin and place ham in a shallow roasting pan. Pour 1½ cups beer over it. Roast in a 375° oven 45 minutes, basting occasionally. Score the fat in any pattern and stud it with cloves. Mix the brown sugar, mustard, and enough of the remaining beer to make a paste and rub it over the ham. Roast 45 minutes longer, or until the ham is glazed and browned. Baste frequently.

One of the best-known recipes from the Scandinavian countries is Sailors' Stew, sometimes known as Sailors' Beef. Its origin goes back many hundreds of years, and it is said that no matter where the ships carried the sailors they prepared their favorite stew. The Norwegians, Swedes, and Danes have traded their own personal variations of the recipe.

SAILORS' STEW

2 pounds beef	1½ teaspoons salt
½ pound calf's or beef liver	¼ teaspoon freshly ground
1 cup thinly sliced onions	black pepper
4 tablespoons butter	¼ teaspoon marjoram
3 cups thinly sliced potatoes	1½ cups beer

Buy beef round or chuck steak. Have it cut ½ inch thick and pound it flat. Cut into strips ½ inch wide by 3 inches long. Cut the liver the same size.

Sauté the onions in 2 tablespoons of the butter 15 minutes, stirring frequently. Remove from pan. Brown the beef and liver in the remaining butter. In a casserole, arrange layers of the meats, onions, and potatoes.

Stir the salt, pepper, marjoram, and beer into the pan. Bring to a boil and scrape the bottom. Pour into the casserole. Cover and bake in a 350° oven 1 hour, removing the cover for the last 10 minutes.

Serves 6–8.

EATING CHINESE FASHION

Chinese food is by far one of the most popular foreign cuisines in the country, proven by the great number of Chinese restaurants all over the United States. It's fun to prepare Chinese food at home too.

Food styles and eating customs vary considerably from one part of China to the other. But there is one thing in common—rice. All the other dishes are intended to supplement the rice.

Texture is very important in the preparation of Chinese dishes. Vegetables are cooked just long enough to make them tender but still crunchy. The shape and size of cut-up foods vary with the individual ingredient to provide different texture. Meat, too, is cooked a short time and is cut up in small pieces, thus eliminating the need for a knife when serving.

Each person is served a bowl of rice and then helps himself from the large bowl of different foods, eating directly from it or transferring the delicacies to his individual rice bowl. Beer is ideal to accentuate the delicious flavors and textures.

For a dinner party or buffet supper, we can deviate slightly in the service but still follow the general Chinese fashion. Serve each of your guests a bowl of rice placed on the center of a large dinner plate. Place bowls of as many different dishes as you want to serve on the table, and your guests may then help themselves. Let them arrange the different foods in small mounds on their own plates, thus adhering to the Chinese custom of using rice as the basis of the meal. A fork and spoon are adequate, but you might like to serve chopsticks. You'll be surprised at how easily you can master their use. Have a few sets of serving spoons available as well as small shallow dishes for sauces and mustard.

In lieu of napkins, small damp, lightly perfumed Turkish towels are provided before dinner, after several courses, and of course at the end of the meal. A simplified method would be to use napkins and then offer the damp towel at the end of the meal—a novel change from a finger bowl.

EGG ROLLS

2 eggs	½ cup cooked ground meat
½ teaspoon salt	or chicken
⅓ cup water	½ cup ground shrimp
½ cup sifted flour	1 teaspoon soy sauce
⅓ cup salad oil	¼ teaspoon pepper
¼ cup sliced scallions (green	½ teaspoon sugar
onions)	Fat for deep frying
2 tablespoons chopped celery	

Any type of leftover meat, poultry, or ham may be used.

Beat together the eggs, salt, water, and flour. Heat 1 tablespoon oil in a 7-inch skillet and pour in just enough batter to coat the bottom. Fry until browned on underside; turn out onto a napkin, browned side up. Continue making the balance, adding oil to the skillet as needed.

Heat 2 tablespoons oil in a skillet; sauté the scallions and celery 3 minutes. Stir in the meat, shrimp, soy sauce, pepper, and sugar. Mix lightly and taste for seasoning.

Place a heaping tablespoon of the mixture on each pancake. Turn opposite sides in and roll up like a jelly roll. Moisten with a little beaten egg yolk to fasten edges. Chill.

Heat the fat (about 3 inches deep) to 360°. Carefully drop the egg rolls into it. Fry until delicately browned on both sides. Drain and serve hot, cut into three, with Chinese mustard.

Makes 6 Egg Rolls.

CHINESE FRIED RICE (*Sub Gum Chow Fan*)

2 cups rice, cooked and drained
3 eggs
3 tablespoons beer
1 cup smoked ham, cut julienne
½ cup diced mushrooms

1 cup coarsely chopped cooked shrimp
1 cup shredded cabbage (Chinese, if available)
⅓ cup peanut or salad oil

Chill the rice for 2 hours.

Beat the eggs and beer together. Stir in the ham, mushrooms, shrimp, and cabbage.

Heat the oil in a large skillet and turn the rice into it. Cook, stirring constantly, until rice is coated with oil. Pour the egg mixture into it and cook, stirring frequently, until rice is browned, about 10 minutes.

Serves 6.

MANDARIN SHRIMP (*Kaik-Jop-Hak-Kow*)

2 pounds raw shrimp
½ cup cornstarch
4 tablespoons salad oil
1 teaspoon powdered ginger
1 clove garlic, minced
½ cup pineapple juice
⅓ cup ketchup

¼ cup water
1 tablespoon vinegar
½ teaspoon Ac'cent
2 tablespoons minced scallions (green onions)
Shredded lettuce

Shell and devein the shrimp, leaving the tail intact; open the shrimp and flatten slightly. Dip in the cornstarch (reserving 2 teaspoons). Heat the oil in a skillet; sauté the shrimp with the ginger and garlic, until delicately browned on both sides. Add the pineapple juice mixed with the ketchup. Cook 3 minutes.

Mix together the remaining cornstarch, the water, Ac'cent, and vinegar; add to the shrimp, stirring constantly to the boiling point. Sprinkle with the scallions and cook 2 minutes.

Heap the lettuce on a serving dish and arrange the shrimp and sauce over it.

Serves 4–6.

SHRIMP EGG FOO YOUNG

1 pound raw shrimp, shelled and deveined

4 tablespoons salad oil

2 tablespoons soy sauce

¼ cup thinly sliced scallions (green onions)

¼ cup thinly sliced celery

½ cup bean sprouts (optional)

8 eggs

2 tablespoons beer

¼ cup water

1 teaspoon salt

Wash, dry, and chop the shrimp. Heat 2 tablespoons oil in a skillet; sauté the shrimp 2 minutes. Stir in the soy sauce, then the scallions, celery, and bean sprouts. Sauté 3 minutes, stirring almost constantly. Remove from heat.

Beat together the eggs, beer, water, and salt. Heat the remaining oil in a 9- or 10-inch skillet. Pour the egg mixture into it. Cook over low heat until partially set. Pour shrimp-vegetable mixture over the eggs and fold the omelet over to cover. Cook until delicately browned on underside, then carefully turn over to brown top. Serves 4.

STEAK AND MUSHROOMS (Moo-Goo-Ngow)

1½ pounds round or sirloin steak

3 tablespoons peanut or salad oil

½ cup diced onions

1 teaspoon minced garlic

1 pound mushrooms, sliced

1 green pepper, thinly sliced

1 teaspoon salt

½ teaspoon Ac'cent

¼ teaspoon pepper

¾ cup beef broth

1 tablespoon cornstarch

1 tablespoon soy sauce

2 tablespoons water

Buy a thin piece of steak and cut it into narrow strips ⅛ inch wide by 3 inches long.

Heat the oil in a large skillet and brown the meat, onions, and garlic, stirring almost constantly. Add the mushrooms and green peppers; cook 2 minutes. Stir in the salt, Ac'cent, pepper, and broth. Cover and cook over low heat 5 minutes, or until meat is tender. Mix together the cornstarch, soy sauce, and water. Blend into the sauce and cook over low heat, stirring constantly to the boiling point. Cook 2 minutes longer and serve with fried noodles or rice. Serves 6.

SWEET AND SOUR MEAT BALLS (*Tin-Shun-Yok-Kow*)

3 green peppers	¾ cup salad oil
1 pound ground beef	1 cup canned pineapple chunks
1½ teaspoon salt	¾ cup beef broth
¼ teaspoon pepper	2 tablespoons cornstarch
¼ teaspoon Ac'cent	1 tablespoon soy sauce
2 tablespoons water	½ cup vinegar
2 tablespoons grated onion	¼ cup sugar
1 egg, beaten	¼ cup pineapple juice
¼ cup flour	

Cut the peppers into 8 wedges, discarding the fibers and seeds. Cover with water; bring to a boil and cook 5 minutes. Drain.

Mix together the beef, salt, pepper, Ac'cent, water, and onion. Shape into 1-inch balls. Dip into the egg and then roll in flour.

Heat the oil in a skillet; fry the meat balls until browned on all sides. Drain and keep warm. Pour off all but 1 tablespoon oil and add the green pepper, pineapple, and broth. Cook over low heat 5 minutes. Mix together the cornstarch, soy sauce, vinegar, sugar, and pineapple juice; add to the skillet, stirring constantly to the boiling point. Cook 5 minutes. Pour over the meat balls. Serves 4.

BAKED CHINESE OMELET

1 cup coarsely chopped mushrooms
3 tablespoons minced onions
2 tablespoons butter
1 tomato, chopped
1 teaspoon salt
¼ teaspoon pepper
½ cup cooked or canned green
peas

1 cup chopped ham
4 egg yolks
½ teaspoon Worcestershire
sauce
½ cup beer
1½ tablespoons cornstarch
4 egg whites, stiffly beaten

Preheat oven to 425°.

Sauté the mushrooms and onions in the butter 5 minutes. Add the tomato, salt, and pepper. Cook over low heat 5 minutes. Stir in the peas and ham. Cool 5 minutes.

Beat the egg yolks, Worcestershire sauce, beer, and cornstarch together. Fold in the egg whites and then the ham mixture. Turn into a buttered 9-inch skillet.

Bake 10 minutes, or until set and browned on top.

Serves 3–4.

SWEET AND PUNGENT PORK (*New-Goo-Yok*)

4 green peppers
2 pounds boneless pork
2 eggs
¼ cup beer
½ cup flour
1 teaspoon salt
¾ cup salad oil
2 cloves minced garlic
1½ cups chicken broth

½ teaspoon ground ginger
3 tablespoons cornstarch
1½ tablespoons soy sauce
¾ cup vinegar
½ cup brown sugar
¾ teaspoon Ac'cent
½ cup pineapple juice
2 cups pineapple chunks

Cut the peppers into 8 pieces, discarding the seeds and fibers. Cover with water; bring to a boil and cook 5 minutes. Drain.

Remove all the fat from the pork; cut the pork into ½-inch cubes. Beat together the eggs, beer, flour, and salt. Dip the pork in the mixture, coating the cubes heavily.

Heat the oil in a large skillet and drop the cubes into it a piece at a time so that each piece rests on the bottom of the skillet. Fry until browned on all sides.

Pour off the fat and add the garlic, ½ cup broth, and the green pepper. Cover and cook over low heat 5 minutes.

Mix together the ginger, cornstarch, soy sauce, vinegar, brown sugar, Ac'cent, pineapple juice, and remaining broth. Add to the pork, stirring constantly to the boiling point. Add the pineapple. Cook 5 minutes.

Serves 6–8.

CHINESE MUSTARD

Mix dry mustard with enough beer to make a smooth paste. Let stand 10 minutes before serving.

SPICY FOODS FROM BELOW THE BORDER

Our neighbors to the south are notoriously fond of spicy, piquant dishes. Simple bland food holds little interest for them, and most Mexican cooks have a heavy, generous hand with hot green and red peppers, chili powder, and other spicy ingredients.

Mexican food has made notable headway in California, New Mexico, Arizona, and Texas, all with borders fronting on to Mexico's. Their dishes have been slightly modified to suit the American palate, and Mexican restaurants are great favorites in those states. Mexican food, it has been noted, calls for thirst-quenching beverages, and there is nothing that can match beer in this respect. So of course there should be large glasses because your guests are surely going to want to drink cooling, refreshing beer with your delicious Mexican dinner.

A Mexican dinner party can be a novel, amusing affair. Use a colored tablecloth, perhaps red or green, and set the table with colored glassware. Arrange fresh fruit, chili peppers, and other raw vegetables around the table in haphazard fashion or in gay pottery bowls. String some peppers on a length of thread and place on the table or hang them from the chandelier or fireplace.

MEXICAN AVOCADO DIP (*Guacamole*)

2 avocados	2 teaspoons salt
3 tomatoes, peeled	1 tablespoon chili powder
¼ cup grated onion	1 tablespoon vinegar
⅛ teaspoon minced garlic	

Perfect party fare. Spicy *Paella* (recipe on page 223) calls for tumblers of refreshing beer or ale.

Cut the avocados in half lengthwise and scoop out the pulp (save 2 halves for serving). Chop the pulp, tomatoes, onion, and garlic to a fine paste (or use the blender). Stir in the salt, chili powder, and vinegar. Taste for seasoning—the mixture should be spicy. Chill and serve in the shell, surrounded by tortillas, corn chips, or potato chips.

Makes about 2½ cups, depending on size of avocados.

RICE AND CLAMS (*Arroz con Almejas*)

36 clams	½ teaspoon freshly ground
3 tablespoons olive oil	black pepper
1 cup rice	2 tablespoons minced parsley
½ cup minced onions	3 tablespoons minced pimientos
2 teaspoons salt	2 tablespoons butter
2 teaspoons chili powder	

Drain the clams, reserving the liquid. Measure the liquid and add enough water to make 4 cups. Coarsely chop the clams.

Heat the oil in a saucepan; add the rice and onions and cook over low heat, stirring frequently until golden brown. Add the 4 cups of liquid, the salt, chili powder, and pepper. Cover and cook over low heat 20 minutes, or until rice is tender and almost dry. Stir in the clams, parsley, pimientos, and butter. Cook 5 minutes.

Serves 4–5.

MEXICAN LAMB STEW

2 pounds boneless lamb	1½ cups beef broth
¼ pound ham	¼ teaspoon dried, ground chili
3 tablespoons olive oil	peppers
½ cup diced onions	Dash ground allspice
2 cups diced potatoes	1 bay leaf
2 cups fresh peas, or frozen, thawed	

Cut the lamb in strips 3 inches by 1 inch. Dice the ham. Brown the lamb and ham in the oil. Add the onions and potatoes and continue browning. Stir in the peas, broth, chili peppers, allspice, and bay leaf. Cover and cook over low heat 45 minutes, or until lamb is tender. (The vegetables should be very soft, so don't worry about overcooking.) Taste for seasoning.

Serves 4–6.

CHILI MEAT LOAF

1 pound ground pork	1 tablespoon chili powder
1 pound ground beef	⅛ teaspoon Tabasco
¼ cup grated onion	2 eggs, beaten
1 clove garlic, minced	¾ cup cracker meal
1½ teaspoons salt	½ cup beer

Mix together all the ingredients except the beer. Press into a greased 9-inch loaf pan. Pour the beer over the top.

Bake in a 375° oven 1¼ hours.

Serves 6.

CHILI DINNER

2 cloves garlic, minced	1 cup diced onions
4 teaspoons salt	1½ cups raw rice, washed and
½ teaspoon pepper	drained
2 pounds round steak cut in 1-	1 pound can kidney beans
inch cubes	1 29-ounce can tomatoes
½ cup olive or salad oil	1 cup sliced black olives
3 tablespoons chili powder	3 cups beef broth

Combine the garlic, 2 teaspoons salt, and the pepper; toss with the meat. Heat half the oil in a skillet and lightly brown the meat. Blend in 1½ tablespoons chili powder. Remove meat. Heat remaining oil and sauté the onions 5 minutes. Add the rice and cook, stirring steadily, until browned. Sprinkle with the remaining salt.

In a casserole, arrange layers of half the meat, the rice sprinkled with chili, beans, canned tomatoes, and olives. Repeat the layers and add the broth. Cover tightly and bake in a 350° oven 1 hour, or until rice and meat are tender. Add more broth if necessary, and taste for seasoning. Serve with tortillas (available in cans or at Mexican restaurants).

Serves 6.

BAKED CHILI CHOPS

½ cup beer	2 tablespoons chili powder
1 cup canned tomato sauce	½ teaspoon ground coriander
2 tablespoons lemon juice	2 cloves minced garlic
1 teaspoon salt	6 loin pork chops

Combine all the ingredients in a bowl; let marinate 3 hours, basting and turning the chops frequently. Arrange the chops in a baking pan; pour the marinade over them.

Bake in a 350° oven 1 hour, turning them after ½ hour. Add a little more beer if pan becomes dry.

Serves 6.

PICKLED FISH (*Pescado en Escabeche*)

4 cups thinly sliced onions	3 tablespoons lime or lemon
1½ cups olive or salad oil	juice
¾ cup cider vinegar	⅓ cup flour
3 teaspoons salt	6 tablespoons butter
2 bay leaves	2 cloves garlic, minced
8 peppercorns, crushed	
6 slices or fillets of white-meat fish	

Combine the onions, oil, vinegar, 1 teaspoon salt, bay leaves, and peppercorns in a saucepan. Bring to a boil and cook over low heat 30 minutes.

Wash and dry the fish. Rub with the lime juice and remaining salt. Lightly dip in the flour. Melt the butter in a skillet and brown the fish and garlic on both sides. Arrange alternate layers of the fish and sauce in a bowl. Cover and let marinate in the refrigerator for at least 24 hours before serving with black olives and tomato wedges. Keeps about 1 week.

Serves 6–12.

TURKEY WITH MOLE SAUCE (*Mole de Guajolote*)

8-pound turkey	2 pounds tomatoes
3 teaspoons salt	½ teaspoon cinnamon
½ cup olive oil	¼ teaspoon dried, ground chili
3 green peppers	peppers
2 tablespoons sesame seeds	2 tablespoons chili powder
6 cloves garlic	2 squares (ounces) unsweet-
4 tortillas or 1 slice toast	ened chocolate, grated
½ cup almonds	

Have the turkey cut up in serving-size pieces. Cook in water to cover, seasoned with 2 teaspoons salt, 1½ hours. Drain, reserving 3 cups stock. Dry the turkey and brown in ¼ cup of the olive oil. Place in a casserole.

Grind together (or run in an electric blender) the green peppers, sesame seeds, garlic, tortillas or toast, almonds, and tomatoes. Blend with cinnamon, chili peppers, chili powder, chocolate, and remaining salt. Cook in the remaining oil 5 minutes, stirring steadily. Blend in the reserved stock and pour over the turkey.

Cover and cook over low heat 1½ hours. Serve with rice.

Serves 8–10.

BEAN CASSEROLE

¾ cup minced onions
2 cloves garlic, minced
½ cup minced green pepper
¼ cup salad oil
2 cups canned tomatoes, drained
2 (20-ounce) cans kidney beans, drained
1 teaspoon salt
¼ teaspoon dried, ground chili peppers
½ teaspoon orégano
3 tablespoons chopped parsley
½ cup grated Cheddar cheese

Sauté the onions, garlic, and green pepper in the oil 10 minutes. Stir in the tomatoes, beans, salt, chili pepper, orégano, and parsley. Turn into a 2-quart casserole. Bake in a 350° oven 45 minutes. Sprinkle with the cheese and bake 10 minutes longer, or until cheese melts and is delicately browned. Serve with cold meats, frankfurters, or hamburgers.
Serves 6.

PUEBLO CASSEROLE

2 cups dried chick-peas (garbanzos, ceci)
1½ pounds Spanish or Italian sausages
2 tablespoons olive oil
1 cup diced onions
1 cup chopped green pepper
2 cloves garlic, minced
1 29-ounce can tomatoes
2 tablespoons chili powder
1 tablespoon minced parsley

Wash the chick-peas. Cover with water and soak overnight; drain. Cover with fresh water and cook until almost tender; drain. (You may use 4 cups canned chick-peas if you prefer, but the flavor is not quite so good.)
Cut the sausages in 2-inch pieces and brown on all sides. Drain. Heat the oil in a casserole and sauté the onions, green pepper, and

garlic 10 minutes. Add the tomatoes, chili powder, and parsley. Cover and cook over low heat 1 hour. Add the sausages and beans. Cover and bake in a 350° oven 1 hour, removing the cover for the last 15 minutes.   Serves 6.

RICE AND CHICK-PEA CASSEROLE (*Arroz con Garbanzos*)

½ pound dried chick-peas or
  3 cups canned
1 pound lean pork
1 cup sliced onions
2 cloves garlic, minced
3 tablespoons olive oil
2 teaspoons salt
½ teaspoon freshly ground
  black pepper

1 teaspoon Spanish paprika
1½ cups raw rice
4 cups chicken broth
2 Spanish or Italian sausages,
  sliced
3 eggs, beaten

Soak the dried chick-peas overnight in water to cover. Drain, add fresh water, and cook 1 hour. Drain.

Cut the pork in narrow strips. Brown the pork, onions, and garlic in the olive oil. Add the salt, pepper, paprika, rice, broth, sausages, and chick-peas. Cover.

Bake in a 375° oven 1 hour. Taste for seasoning. Gently mix the eggs in and bake uncovered until eggs set, about 10 minutes. Serves 6.

TAMALE PIE

¼ cup flour
2 teaspoons salt
¼ teaspoon pepper
1 teaspoon chili powder
1½ pounds beef, diced
3 tablespoons olive oil

½ cup minced onions
1 cup beer
½ cup condensed tomato soup
1 cup corn kernels
3 tablespoons minced parsley
Corn-bread mix

Combine flour, salt, pepper, and chili powder on a piece of waxed paper. Roll the meat in it.

Heat the oil in a deep skillet and brown the meat and onions. Stir in the beer and tomato soup. Cover and cook over low heat 45 minutes, or until tender. Add the corn and parsley. Turn into a casserole or deep pie plate.

Follow instructions on package of corn-bread mix and cover the casserole with it.

Bake in a 350° oven 35 minutes, or until browned.

Serves 6.

PAELLA

1 (3-pound) frying chicken, cut up	1½ cups beer
1¼ teaspoons salt, divided	1½ cups broth
½ teaspoon paprika	½ teaspoon Tabasco
4 tablespoons cooking oil or butter	¼ teaspoon saffron
½ pound ham, diced	1½ cups raw rice
1 medium onion, choppped	6 mussels
½ cup diced green pepper	6 clams
1 can (1 pound) peas	½ pound shrimp, cooked and cleaned
	2 pimientos, cut in pieces

Sprinkle chicken with 1 teaspoon of salt and paprika. Heat oil in skillet; brown chicken; remove to baking dish with tight-fitting lid. Cook ham in skillet; add to chicken.

Cook onion and green pepper until onion is tender. Stir the beer, broth, and Tabasco into skillet, scraping brown particles from bottom of pan. Add saffron and remaining ¼ teaspoon salt. Bring to a boil; pour over chicken and ham. Sprinkle rice over chicken; stir so all of rice is moistened. Cover tightly. Bake in 350° oven 25 minutes. Uncover; toss rice.

Arrange mussels and clams on top of rice with shrimp, pimientos, and peas. Cover; return to oven 10 minutes longer.

Serves 6.

A JAPANESE HIBACHI PARTY

Japanese food is blander than Chinese but has many points of interest for Westerners. In Japan even greater emphasis is placed upon appearance than in China. Each dish is treated as a work of art; sometimes the food is presented so attractively that eating the arrangement seems almost like the desecration of a masterpiece.

Charcoal is the universal fuel, and cooking centers around a cast-iron brazier, the *hibachi*, now available here. Of course a chafing dish, electric skillet, or outdoor grill may also be used. Beer is the ideal beverage, as next to *sake* (rice wine) it is the favorite drink in Japan.

The usual festive meal begins with fish or seafood, proceeds to sukiyaki made with beef, pork, or chicken, accompanied by rice or vermicelli-type noodles, raw vegetables dressed with sweetened vinegar, and ends with fruit, fresh or preserved. To carry out the Japanese theme, arrange a few flowers in the Japanese manner, use gaily decorated china, and, if you like, serve the food with chopsticks.

BAKED CLAMS AND PEAS (*Omukò-kaimori*)

24 clams or 3 7½-ounce cans minced clams
Chicken broth
1 tablespoon cornstarch
2 teaspoons soy sauce

¼ cup minced scallions (green onions)
1 cup cooked or canned tiny green peas

Scrub the clams and open them. Reserve the shells. Measure the juice and add enough broth to make 1 cup. Chop the clams.

Mix together the cornstarch and broth. Cook over low heat, stirring constantly until thickened. Stir in the soy sauce, scallions, peas, and clams. Fill the shells if fresh clams were used or divide the mixture among 6 ramekins.

Bake in a 425° oven 10 minutes. Serve hot.

Serves 6.

LOBSTER, TEMPURA STYLE

3 lobsters or 6 frozen lobster	½ cup beer
tails	1½ cups sifted flour
6 eggs	Fat for deep frying

If lobsters are used, have them split and the claws and feelers removed. (Use for salad.) If frozen lobster tails are used, thaw them. Leave the meat in the shells, but make a few cuts in the meat to allow the batter to enter.

Beat the eggs, beer, and flour together. Dip the lobsters in the mixture, coating them thoroughly.

Heat the fat to 350°. Fry two pieces of lobster at a time until browned, about 10 minutes. Drain and keep warm while preparing the balance. Serve with the following sauce:

¾ cup beef consommé	1 teaspoon ground ginger
¼ cup soy sauce	½ cup grated horseradish or
½ cup beer	turnip

Combine the consommé, soy sauce, beer, and ginger in a saucepan. Bring to a boil. Cool. Serve the sauce in individual dishes with a spoon of horseradish or turnip in the center. The lobster is then dipped into it.

Serves 3–6.

Note: Shrimp may be prepared in the same manner.

JAPANESE OMELET

1 cup tuna fish, crab meat, or cooked shrimp	2 teaspoons sugar
4 eggs	¾ teaspoon salt
¼ cup beer	3 tablespoons grated onion
1 tablespoon flour	2 tablespoons salad oil

Mash or chop the fish very fine. Beat the eggs, beer, flour, sugar, salt, and onion together. Stir in the fish.

Heat 1 tablespoon oil in a 9-inch skillet. Pour half of the mixture into it. Cook over low heat until set on the underside. Turn over and cook until lightly browned. Slide out and roll up like a jelly roll. Repeat with balance of mixture.

Serves 2.

Note: Small versions, cooked in 6- or 7-inch skillets, are delicious as an appetizer.

SUKIYAKI

Sukiyaki may be prepared with any combination of vegetables and with beef, chicken, or pork. The one important factor is texture. Don't overcook the vegetables—they should be slightly crunchy when eaten. In the Japanese style, you can cook the Sukiyaki at the table in a chafing dish or electric skillet. If you like, cut the ingredients earlier in the day and wrap them in foil or waxed paper until needed.

½ cup beer	3 large onions, sliced thin
¼ cup beef consommé	1 cup sliced celery
½ cup soy sauce	¼ pound mushrooms, sliced
3 tablespoons sugar	1 cup sliced bamboo shoots
½ teaspoon Ac'cent	1 cup shredded spinach
2 pounds sirloin or round steak	8 scallions (green onions),
4 tablespoons peanut or salad oil	sliced

Combine the beer, consommé, soy sauce, sugar, and Ac'cent. Cut the steak cross-grain into paper-thin slices.

Heat the oil in a skillet; brown the steak. Push to one side and pour ¼ cup of the beer mixture over it. Add the onions, celery, and mushrooms to the skillet; sauté 3 minutes. Add the remaining beer mixture, bamboo shoots, and spinach. Cook over low heat 3 minutes. Sprinkle the scallions over all and cook 2 minutes.

Sukiyaki is customarily served with *udon*—a thin noodle. Vermicelli or fine noodles are a good substitute.

Serves 6.

MARINATED STEAK (*Teriyaki*)

3 pounds fillet of beef	4 tablespoons brown sugar
1 cup soy sauce	2 tablespoons grated onion
⅓ cup beer	2 cloves garlic, minced
2 teaspoons ground ginger	2 teaspoons cornstarch

Have the fillet cut in 4 pieces lengthwise. Combine the soy sauce, beer, ginger, brown sugar, onion, and garlic in a bowl (not metal). Marinate the steak 3 hours.

Remove the steak from the marinade and place on an oiled rack. Broil in a hot broiler (or over a charcoal fire) 7–10 minutes, or to the desired degree of rareness. Turn frequently.

Mix together the cornstarch and marinade. Cook over low heat, stirring constantly until thickened. Slice the steak crosswise and serve with the sauce.

Serves 6–8.

AN ITALIAN FRITTO MISTO
PARTY

The selection of foods served in a Fritto Misto differs from city to city in Italy. Rome uses fish as the basic ingredient, whereas in Milan liver, sweetbreads, and brains are the chief ingredients. In addition there are eggplant fingers, sliced zucchini, tiny whole artichokes, cauliflowerets, and potato croquettes. Arrange each food on a serving dish, with lemon wedges and parsley around it. This presentation makes an unusual delicious antipasto, buffet supper, or seated dinner.

Cut the fish in sticks or squares. Use cleaned raw shrimp, whole small smelts or whiting, and clams. Dip in Fritter Batter and fry in deep fat until delicately browned. Use the freshest calf's liver cut in 2-inch strips, or chicken livers cut in half. Dip in the Fritter Batter and fry. The brains and sweetbreads should be parboiled and cut in 4 before being dipped in the batter.

Buy the smallest artichokes you can find and cut off the tips. Remove the tough outer leaves. Spread the artichokes open and remove the spiny choke from the center. Wash the artichokes in cold water mixed with a little lemon juice. Drain and season with salt and pepper. Fry the artichokes in deep fat (olive oil preferably) for about 10 minutes. Drain on paper towels, then chill for 2 hours. Heat fat to 385°. Hold the artichoke with a fork inserted in the stem end and plunge it into the fat. The artichoke will open like a flower and each leaf will be as crisp as a potato chip.

Peeled, uncooked eggplant fingers, unpeeled sliced zucchini, and cauliflowerets are dipped in Fritter Batter and fried in deep fat heated to 370°.

You may also have bowls of spicy peperoni (tiny green peppers) and *Caponata* to supply the spice for the Fritto Misto. Garlic or toasted cheese bread are also delicious. Chill the beer in ice-filled bowls placed in wicker baskets.

For dessert, a frozen light Biscuit Tortoni is ideal.

ITALIAN VEGETABLE RELISH (*Caponata*)

4 cups diced eggplant	⅓ cup wine vinegar
½ cup olive oil	2 teaspoons sugar
1 cup chopped green pepper	2 tablespoons tomato paste
1 cup diced celery	¾ cup water
¾ cup minced onion	½ cup chopped green olives
1 clove garlic, minced	1 tablespoon capers
1½ teaspoons salt	1 tablespoon minced parsley
¼ teaspoon freshly ground	
black pepper	

Sauté the eggplant in 3 tablespoons olive oil 10 minutes, stirring frequently. Remove. Sauté the green pepper and celery in 2 tablespoons olive oil 5 minutes. Remove. Sauté the onion in the remaining oil 5 minutes. Add the garlic, salt, pepper, vinegar, sugar, tomato paste, and water. Cover and cook over low heat 10 minutes. Add the olives, capers, parsley, and sautéed vegetables. Cover and cook 15 minutes. Taste for seasoning and chill.

Makes about 3 cups.

NEAPOLITAN STUFFED PEPPERS

6 green or red peppers	3 tablespoons capers
½ cup olive oil	½ cup sliced black olives
½ cup finely chopped onions	¼ teaspoon orégano
½ cup chopped mushrooms	2 tablespoons tomato paste
2 cups soft bread crumbs	2 tablespoons water
6 anchovies, shredded	

Cut a 1-inch piece from the stem end of the peppers. Scoop out the seeds and fibers.

Heat half the oil in a skillet and sauté the onions and mushrooms 5 minutes. Stir in the bread crumbs, anchovies, capers, olives, orégano, tomato paste, and water. Stuff the peppers loosely.

Arrange peppers in an upright position in a baking dish. Brush with the remaining oil.

Bake in a 350° oven 45 minutes, or until peppers are tender.

You may also baste the peppers with 1½ cups of canned tomatoes, if desired. Taste the sauce for seasoning before serving. Serve hot or cold.

Serves 6.

BAKED CLAMS ARIGANATA

2 cloves garlic, minced
½ teaspoon orégano
2 tablespoons minced parsley
1½ teaspoons salt
½ teaspoon freshly ground
    black pepper
¾ cup dry bread crumbs
¼ cup olive oil
36 clams on the half shell

Mix to a paste the garlic, orégano, parsley, salt, pepper, bread crumbs, and oil. Spread on the clams.

Fill a shallow baking pan with rock salt or crumpled aluminum foil. Arrange the clams on it. Bake in a 450° oven 5 minutes. Serve with lemon wedges.

POTATO CROQUETTES

4 potatoes (1½ pounds)
2 egg yolks
⅓ cup grated Parmesan cheese
1 teaspoon salt
⅛ teaspoon white pepper
1½ tablespoons minced parsley
½ cup dry bread crumbs
Fat for deep frying

Cook the unpeeled potatoes until tender. Peel and mash. Beat in the egg yolks, cheese, salt, pepper, and parsley. Make into rolls 2½ inches long and 1 inch thick. Roll in the bread crumbs.

Heat the fat to 375° and fry the croquettes until browned.

ROLLATINE OF BEEF

2 pounds sirloin steak	1½ cups beer
1 cup dry bread crumbs	¼ cup flour
6 slices bacon, half cooked, drained and crumbled	1½ teaspoons salt
	½ teaspoon pepper
1 teaspoon prepared mustard	2 tablespoons olive or salad oil
2 tablespoons melted butter	2 onions, sliced
1 tablespoon minced parsley	¼ teaspoon thyme

Have the meat cut thin and pounded as thin as possible. Cut in 6 oblong pieces. Mix together the bread crumbs, bacon, mustard, butter, and parsley. Add just enough beer to moisten the mixture. Spread on the steak and roll up tightly. Tie with thread. Mix the flour with a little salt and pepper; roll the roulades in it.

Heat the oil in a skillet; brown the onions and roulades. Add the remaining beer, salt, and pepper, and the thyme. Cover and cook over low heat 1 hour, or until tender. Turn the roulades twice during the cooking time.

Serves 6.

CLAM SOUP (Zuppa de Vongole)

3 dozen little-neck clams	½ cup water
¾ cup olive oil	3 tablespoons minced parsley
2 anchovy fillets, chopped	½ teaspoon salt
2 cloves garlic, minced	½ teaspoon freshly ground black pepper
1 cup beer	
3 tablespoons tomato paste	

Wash and scrub the clams. Heat the oil in a saucepan; sauté the anchovies and garlic 2 minutes. Add the beer, tomato paste, water, parsley, salt, and pepper. Bring to a boil and cook over low heat 10 minutes. Add the clams and cook until the shells open, about 5 minutes. Serve in soup plates.

Serves 2 generously or 4 adequately.

ITALIAN BEEF PIE

1½ pounds ground beef
2 teaspoons salt
½ teaspoon freshly ground black pepper
2 teaspoons prepared mustard
1 teaspoon Worcestershire sauce
1 20-ounce can tomatoes, drained

2 tablespoons olive oil
3 tablespoons grated onion
1 cup (¼ pound) Mozzarella cheese, diced
½ teaspoon orégano
⅛ teaspoon dried, ground chili peppers
2 tablespoons minced parsley

Mix together the beef, salt, pepper, mustard, and Worcestershire sauce. Line a 9-inch pie plate with the mixture. Spread the tomatoes in it and sprinkle with the oil, onion, cheese, orégano, chili peppers, and parsley.

Bake in a 375° oven 25 minutes. Cut in wedges and serve hot. Serves 4–6.

VEAL CACCIATORE

1½ pounds round or loin of veal
½ cup flour
1 teaspoon salt
¼ teaspoon pepper
4 tablespoons olive oil

½ pound mushrooms, sliced
½ cup beer
1 clove garlic, minced
3 tomatoes, peeled and chopped
2 tablespoons minced parsley

Have the veal cut very thin and in serving-size pieces. Flatten the veal by pounding it between 2 sheets of waxed paper (or have the butcher do it).

Mix together the flour, salt, and pepper; dip the veal in the mixture, coating both sides.

Heat the oil in a skillet and brown the veal. Remove and keep warm. Sauté the mushrooms in the same skillet; return the veal to the skillet and add the beer, garlic, and tomatoes. Cook over low heat 10 to 15 minutes. Taste for seasoning and sprinkle with parsley.

Serves 6.

BISCUIT TORTONI

2 egg yolks	1 cup cream, whipped
4 tablespoons sugar	¾ cup macaroon crumbs or
½ cup beer	ground almonds
2 egg whites	

Beat the egg yolks; add 2 tablespoons sugar and the beer. Place over hot water and cook, stirring constantly until thickened. Cool.

Beat the egg whites until they begin to stiffen, then beat in remaining sugar until stiff but not dry. Fold into the yolk mixture with the whipped cream and ¼ cup crumbs or almonds. Spoon into 12 2½-inch paper cups or turn into refrigerator trays. Sprinkle with remaining crumbs or nuts. Freeze until firm.

Makes 12.

Beer Drinks

BEER DRINKS

Beer has been the beverage served at festive occasions back to Babylonian days. It is said to have been called "the nectar of the gods" in early Greece. Beer was served to the heroes of Valhalla as a most worthy reward.

Through the ages various countries have developed their own drinking habits. In Germany there are beer festivals lasting weeks. Beer is served at christening parties in the north countries as the favorite beverage. Australia and Africa have an hour before dinner called "the sundowner" and almost everyone drinks beer, plain or mixed. In Africa it is not unusual to see women and men order a 2-quart bottle of beer for individual consumption.

Beer is a friendly beverage and combines well with other ingredients to create exciting, delicious drinks.

BREWER'S COFFEE

Prepare the coffee as you usually do, brewed drip or vacuum method or instant—but use beer in place of water. Use sugar if you like, and serve hot or iced in old-fashioned glasses with whipped cream. A delicious exotic drink, easily prepared, and one that will pique the taste buds of your guests.

During the Seventeenth century an important English custom arose of drinking to the health of one's guests especially during Christmas Eve and Twelfth-night festivities. Upon the arrival of a guest, the host handed him a mug of spiced ale and said "Wassail," meaning "Be healthy," from the Middle English expression *waes hael*. The guest customarily responded by bowing to his host and answering, "*Drink hael*," or "Drink in good health."

In many small British communities the local townsfolk would go into the orchards and drink a "wassail" to the apple trees to assure their future abundance. Thus it has become customary to decorate the wassail bowl with apples, symbolic of the old Anglo-Saxon practice.

WASSAIL BOWL

8 very small apples
8 teaspoons brown sugar
4 cups ale
¼ teaspoon ground nutmeg
½ teaspoon ground cinnamon
¼ teaspoon ground ginger
½ cup granulated sugar
1½ cups dry sherry (fino or amontillado)

Core the apples carefully and fill each with a teaspoon of brown sugar. Place in a baking pan and cover the bottom with very little water. Bake in a 350° oven until tender, about 35 minutes.

In a saucepan, heat the ale, nutmeg, cinnamon, ginger, sugar, and sherry. Stir until sugar is dissolved. Cook over low heat 15 minutes, but do not let the mixture boil. Pour the ale mixture into a punch bowl and decorate with the baked apples. Serve in pewter tankards or stone mugs.

Serves about 8.

Note: If you like, instead of using baked apples, try tiny, spiced crab apples.

In the England of Dickens' times a posset was the drink to have when one felt tired or had a cold. The novels of a century ago had heroines who often felt the need of a posset in moments of stress. A posset, formerly called a "poshote" during Chaucer's day, is in

*reality any hot drink curdled with beer or ale. Even now when
something curdles while cooking it is not unusual to hear someone
say that "it curdled like a posset."*

ALE POSSET

4 tablespoons brown sugar   4 eggs
1 quart ale   2 slices toast cut into small
3 whole cloves   stars, squares, etc.
¼ teaspoon ground cinnamon

Heat the sugar, ale, cloves, and cinnamon, but do not let the
mixture boil. Discard the cloves.

Beat the eggs in a bowl. Gradually add some of the ale mixture,
stirring steadily. Return mixture to the heat, stirring steadily. If
possible, place some of the mixture in an electric blender until
foamy, or beat with a rotary beater. Serve hot in mugs. Decorate
each with a small piece of toast.

Serves about 8.

*A Christmas Eve custom in the England of a century ago was to
offer each guest a posset cup and a piece of apple pie or tart. Then
on to the next house for more Christmas carols and more apple pie!*

OLD-FASHIONED POSSET

4 cups milk   1 teaspoon cinnamon
4 tablespoons sugar   4 cups ale or beer
4 slices toast

Heat the milk, sugar, and toast in a saucepan, but don't let it
boil. Stir the cinnamon and beer together in a punch bowl.

Discard the toast. Pour the hot milk over the ale and stir. Drink
from mugs while warm.

Serves 8–10.

SHERRY POSSET

2 slices toast, trimmed	4 cups beer
1 tablespoon sugar	2 cups sherry (fino or amontil-
1 tablespoon cinnamon	lado)

Butter the toast and sprinkle with the sugar and cinnamon; press the mixture into the toast. Cut into 8 pieces.

Place the toast, beer, and sherry in a saucepan and heat, but do not allow to boil. Serve while hot.

Serves 8.

*   *   *

The expression about minding your P's and Q's probably originated in the England of several centuries ago. It was customary to mark on the wall the various pints and quarts consumed by the customers who spent an evening at the ale house.

*   *   *

A syllabub is a type of milk punch and is very refreshing on a warm day. It is a mild drink when made with sweet cider but changes its character if hard cider is used.

SYLLABUS

½ cup currants or seedless
   raisins
2 cups beer
2 cups cider

1½ quarts milk
½ teaspoon ground nutmeg or
   cinnamon

Pour boiling water over the currants or raisins and let stand 30 minutes.

Combine the beer, cider, and milk; chill. When cold, beat the mixture with a rotary beater until foamy. Pour into a punchbowl. Drain the currants or raisins and sprinkle over the mixture. Taste the Syllabub; it may need a little sugar, depending upon the cider used. Sprinkle with the cinnamon.

ONE YARD OF FLANNEL

¼ cup sugar
4 tablespoons cognac
3 egg yolks

3 egg whites
2 cups ale
½ teaspoon grated nutmeg

Before you start, make sure you have two large pitchers available.

Combine the sugar and cognac and stir together until fairly smooth. Beat the egg yolks until light in color. Beat the egg whites until stiff but not dry. Place the ale in a saucepan and heat until it barely begins to boil, and then add the sugar mixture. Remove from the heat.

Add the beaten egg yolks, egg whites, and nutmeg and stir together. Pour into one of the pitchers. Pour from one pitcher to another *carefully*, but with some speed, so as to induce the mixture to foam. The drink should be quite smooth.

Purl is a beer drink with an old history and with dozens of different variations. This is one English version particularly suitable for a cold winter's day.

PURL

1 cup beer or ale
1 ounce gin
Dash bitters

Heat the beer until it boils. In a mug or stein, combine the gin and bitters. Pour the beer over it.

DOG'S NOSE

1½ jiggers (ounces) gin
1 cup chilled beer

Combine the gin and beer.

LAMB'S WOOL

1 cup applesauce
2 cups ale

¼ teaspoon vanilla extract
¼ teaspoon powdered ginger

Combine the applesauce and ale in a saucepan and heat; remove from the heat just before the boiling point. Add the vanilla extract and ginger and stir well. Taste; you might want to add a little sugar if the applesauce is unsweetened. Drink while hot.

Here is a cold-weather drink that is popular in Russia when the ground is covered with snow and the wind whistles across the steppes:

RUSSIAN ZBEETIN

1 cup beer
1 teaspoon honey

Heat the beer and honey in a saucepan, but don't let it boil. Serve in glasses.

BISHOP

8 whole cloves	4 cups ale
2 large oranges	1 tablespoon brown sugar

Place 4 cloves in each orange. Bake in a 250° oven until very soft, about 25 minutes. Heat the ale and sugar together in a saucepan. Cut each orange into 4 pieces and discard the seeds; add to the beer mixture. Remove from heat and let stand 30 minutes.

Heat again, but do not allow to boil. Serve hot with a piece of orange in each stone mug or punch-bowl cup.   Serves 4–6.

OGGE (*Danish Beer Toddy*)

1½ cups beer	2 tablespoons brown sugar
2 egg yolks	

Heat the beer, but do not allow it to boil. Beat the egg yolks and sugar in a bowl until light in color. Gradually add a little of the hot beer, stirring constantly. Return the mixture to the saucepan, stirring steadily. Reheat, but do not allow to boil.

If you like, sprinkle a little grated nutmeg on top of each serving. Serves 2.

MULLED ALE OR BEER

1 teaspoon honey	¼ teaspoon grated nutmeg
1 cup ale or beer	

Place the honey in the bottom of a stone mug. Heat the ale or beer in a saucepan, but do not allow it to boil. Pour over the honey and sprinkle with the nutmeg.

If you wish, make your Mulled Ale in the traditional fashion. Wash a poker or rod carefully. Heat it until red hot. Immerse it slowly and carefully into the mug containing the honey and ale, being careful not to let it overflow.

BUL (*a favorite drink in the West Indies*)

3 tablespoons sugar	1 cup beer, chilled
3 tablespoons fresh lemon or lime juice	2 cups carbonated water, chilled

Dissolve the sugar in the lemon or lime juice; pour into a large pitcher. Add the beer and carbonated water and some ice cubes. Mix together. Decorate with thin slices of lemon or lime.

SPICED BEER

4 cups beer	¼ teaspoon ground cinnamon
¾ cup cognac	3 whole cloves
1 tablespoon sugar	¼ teaspoon nutmeg
2 eggs	

Cool the beer and cognac.

Combine the beer and cognac in a bowl. Add the sugar. Beat the eggs well. Add with the cinnamon, cloves, and nutmeg; mix together until well blended. Also called "Huckle-My-Buff" in England.

CRAMBAMBULL EGG NOG

1 cup rum	3 cups beer
½ cup sugar	4 eggs

Combine the rum, sugar, and beer in a saucepan. Bring to a boil and cook 5 minutes. Remove from the heat. Beat the eggs in a bowl; gradually add the beer mixture, stirring steadily to prevent curdling. Allow to chill in the refrigerator at least 2 hours.

Before serving, place in an electric blender until foamy or beat with a rotary beater. If you like a rich egg nog, add ½ cup sweet cream before beating.

One of the classic favorites in England for many years.

HALF AND HALF (*also known as 'Arf 'n' 'Arf*)

1 cup beer, chilled
1 cup ale, chilled

Pour the beer and ale into one glass. Particularly good in stone mugs or pewter tankards.

Any combination of two types of beer, ale, porter, or stout will make a good drink. Experiment until you find a combination that pleases you.

Brown Betty is an old English drink, delicious served at an afternoon tea as a refreshing change from the inevitable cake and coffee. It's equally delightful at an evening party. Serve wedges of cheese and crisp crackers with it.

BROWN BETTY

1 cup cognac	3 cloves
4 cups beer	¼ cup brown sugar
¼ teaspoon cinnamon	2 cups water

Combine all the ingredients and mix well. Chill for 2 hours before serving.

Serves 6–8.

SHANDY GAFF

    1 cup beer, chilled
    1 cup ginger ale, chilled

Pour the beer and ginger ale simultaneously into a champagne or beer glass. The drink will taste even better if the glass has been previously chilled in the refrigerator.

This recipe is adapted from the English Shandy Gaff, which uses ginger beer, usually unobtainable in the United States. If you can find some, use it in place of the ginger ale.

VODKA AND BEER

    1 ounce (jigger) vodka
    1 cup beer, chilled

Combine the vodka and beer. If you like, add a paper-thin slice of lemon on top.

Beer at its Best

A FEW THOUGHTS ABOUT BUYING STORING AND SERVING BEER

Most people know that wine must be treated with care, but comparatively few recognize that beer, too, requires proper handling. By following these suggestions you will find that beer at its best will be even more delightful than you anticipated.

STORING BEER: Any cool, *dark* place is suitable. Beer leaves the brewery in perfect condition for drinking; exposure to sunlight or extremes of heat or cold (all of which would adversely affect it) must be avoided. The riboflavin contained in beer is destroyed by exposure to direct sunlight, causing a peculiar "baked" taste. Keep stored beer out of direct light, particularly sunlight, and of course don't purchase bottles that have been displayed in a shopwindow. Naturally your storage place will not be near furnaces, hot-water pipes, or ovens (or in sun-baked garages).

STORAGE TIME: For the utmost in pleasure, drink beer shortly after it is purchased. Don't age beer—it doesn't improve with time and will never be better than the day it is brought into your home. Experts agree that beer should not be stored longer than ninety days, preferably less.

COOLING: The best place to cool beer and thus have it available for general use is on the bottom shelf of the refrigerator. This *dry cold* method keeps beer at the correct temperature, always ready for drinking. A quick way to chill beer is with *wet cold*—a cooler or bucket filled with ice cubes and cold water. Another method that cannot be wholeheartedly recommended (but may be used in emergencies) is to chill the bottles or cans in a home freezer; wait about 5 minutes and then turn the containers over. In no event should the beer remain in the freezer for more than 15 minutes. Above all, don't freeze cans of beer to take along to the beach or for a picnic; your beer will be barely drinkable, an example of beer at its worst. Above all, never add ice directly to beer.

Once beer has been chilled, it should not be returned to room temperature. If chilled beer is not used, don't remove it from the refrigerator. Store it there until required, for the change to room temperature will harm its delicate flavor.

SERVING TEMPERATURE: In England and Germany many beers are served at or close to room temperature, far too warm for American tastes. On the other hand, all impartial experts agree that American beer is invariably served much too cold, often bordering on the frigid. From 42° to 45° is the correct range; it is then that beer sparkles, exhilarating and delighting the palate. Under 42° the pristine clarity of the beverage is impaired, the aroma is withheld, and the tiny, effervescent bubbles are repressed because of the extreme cold. Over 45° a certain liveliness of taste inherent in beer vanishes and its clean, crisp taste seems flattened out. At the warmer temperatures, the gases are released far too quickly and there is excessive foam. At the correct temperatures (between 42° and 45°), the head or foam on the beer will bear the proper proportion to the liquid. The volatile gases will break through properly (neither too fast nor too slow), offering a delightful fillip to the drinker.

Naturally no one except a perfectionist would bother to put a thermometer into each glass of beer to check the temperature. However, there is an easier way. Place a thermometer on the bottom shelf of your refrigerator, the recommended cooling place. If your refrigerator is operating properly, the temperature should read about 42°. Beer stored in this location will have the same temperature and be ideal for drinking. If it is colder or warmer, a slight adjustment of the thermostatic control will bring your refrigerator to the correct temperature.

OPENING BOTTLES AND CANS: Before opening, don't shake or agitate the container. Excessive motion causes the beer to become "wild"—with too much foam and too little liquid; often the contents will spout like an uncontrolled oil gusher.

Bottles: Don't ease the cap off. Hold the bottle securely about the neck with the left hand; using firm pressure, lift the cap off with one steady motion.

Cans: Use a scrupulously clean can opener, preferably one that is used only for beer. The metal must not bear any rust marks. Press the opener down firmly and decisively so as to barely puncture the can, making only a pin-point hole. Wait about one second for the pressure to equalize, then continue pressing down to create a larger opening in the can suitable for pouring. If you like, repeat the process on the opposite side of the can, but there will be a slightly better head with just one opening.

* * *

The Romans knew how to make glass, and during their invasion of Britain, beer was served in glass containers. When the Roman occupation ended, glassware became scarce. The hard-pressed Britains invented a container made of leather and so constructed that when placed upon a table it would "tumble" over since the bottom was rounded. Therefore, the entire contents had to be consumed at a single draught. Today we drink from "tumblers," too, but ours have a flat bottom.

* * *

GLASSWARE: Over the centuries that beer has been popular, many different types of glasses have come into use. Actually, almost any clear glass is suitable. Here are some of the most acclaimed types, particularly suited for the full enjoyment of beer:

Glassware may be washed by hand or in an electric dishwasher, but in any event should be immaculately clean. Soap is unsatisfactory as a cleansing agent; the fat leaves invisible traces on the glass (no matter how carefully rinsed), and this affects the head on the beer. A detergent, salt, or baking-soda solution is much more suitable, for none of these contains undesirable fats. If for any reason cleansing with soap seems desirable, then wash afterward with detergent, salt, or soda solution. Don't dry the glasses; turn them upside down to drain. Always serve beer in wet glasses to maintain its maximum effervescence. If the glassware is completely dry, rinse the inside with cold water and then gently shake away the excess. This procedure prevents bubbles from forming on the sides of the glass which would inhibit the formation of a proper head when the beer is poured. Don't use glasses for beer that have been used for milk or sweet carbonated beverages.

In addition to glass drinking utensils, a variety of stone, china, and pewter mugs are fancied by many people. As a rule, these are better with the heavier-bodied and sweeter beers, such as ale. Mugs with lids tend to retard disintegration of the bubbles, an advantage to those who linger over their drinks.

How to Pour: Once the container is opened, pour the contents out without delay, but *slowly* and *deliberately*. Fast pouring causes foam to build up rapidly, thus resulting in an overfilled glass.

There are three schools of thought on how to pour beer:

(a) Tilt glass to an angle of 45°. Raise container to 90° and pour beer gently down the side of the glass. When nearly half filled, raise bottle or can directly over the center of the glass, as shown, and pour. Be careful not to overfill the glass.

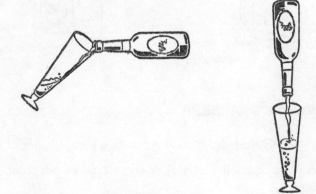

(b) With glass upright, hold bottle or can at angle shown and pour beer down side of glass slowly in order to build head of proper depth.

(c) Hold bottle upside down over center of good-sized flat-bottomed mug or hollow-stemmed goblet. Let good head form to reduce carbonation. As head diminishes, add remaining beer. Do not try to empty bottle or can in first pouring.

THE ABC'S OF BEER

Aroma – delightfully fresh and light, with a pleasing odor of hops.

Bubbles – quite small and very lively, a type of pin-point effervescence.

Color – amber, ranging from a light to fairly deep color, depending upon the nature of the brew.

Collar of foam – rich, heavily textured, and thick; about one inch in height is right.

Cleanliness and brilliance – fine beer seems to sparkle.

FOREIGN BEER TERMS

PORTUGAL	*Cerveja*	DENMARK	*Öl*
SPAIN	*Cerveza*	HOLLAND	*Bier*
FRANCE	*Bière*	GERMANY	*Bier*
BELGIUM	*Bière*	CZECHOSLOVAKIA	*Pivo*
ITALY	*Birra*	POLAND	*Piwo*
FINLAND	*Olutta*	HUNGARY	*Sör*
NORWAY	*Öll*	JAPAN	*Biru*
SWEDEN	*Öl*		

INDEX